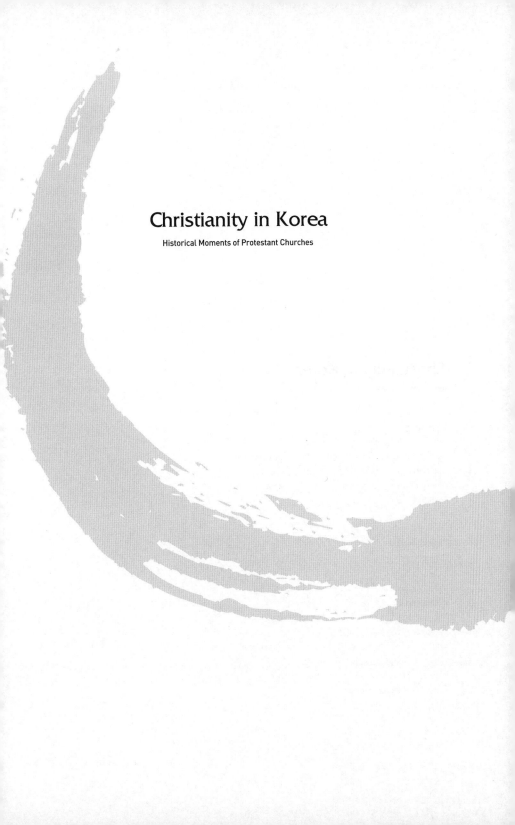

Christianity in Korea

Historical Moments of Protestant Churches

Christianity in Korea

Historical Moments of Protestant Churches

Written by

Lim Heekuk(The chief writer/ Prof. at PCTS)

Kang Hyunsun   Kim Youngmyeong   Park Jonghyun
Son Seungho   Song Hyeonkang   Lee Yongmin
Lee Chiman   Jeon Insoo   Jeong Junho
Hwang Misook

Translated by

Chung Jujin

Published by

The National Council of Churches in Korea
Telephone: 82-2-763-7323
Address: Rm. 706, Korea Christian Bldg. 19 Daehak-ro,
         Jongno, Seoul 110-736, Korea
Website: http://www.kncc.or.kr/
E-mail: kncc@kncc.or.kr

Christianity in Korea

Historical Moments of Protestant Churches

Preface

It has been 130 years since Protestantism first arrived in Korea. Christian communities in the early years were very small and yet they had to endure many difficulties as they faced the turbulent Korean history. Churches struggled with how to live as God's body. Churches were religiously awakened and followed their religious insights. Churches could become good friends to Koreans in suffering and despair.

In 1905, the General Council of Evangelical Missions decided to establish one Korean Christ church. This was one of the most important historical moments in Korean Protestant history. The accomplishment of this great dream took a long time. The Korea National Christian Council was eventually founded in 1924. The Christian values the organization embraced at that time were passed down to the Christians of our time.

Churches have achieved remarkable growth when you compare them to the first churches in the late nineteenth century and the early twentieth century. The first Christian communities' small but significant histories of being light and salt have unfortunately faded away with the churches' rapid growth. The history of Korean Christians' faith that was planted and grown with tears is being forgotten as the small, beautiful churches in the countryside that used to be a strong presence in our lives are disappearing.

The NCCK published the book, *Christianity in Korea: One Hundred Stories of Protestant Churches*, to keep the precious history of the churches that make our current existence possible and further, to lay a foundation for the churches of the future. In particular, the NCCK publishes its English version, *Christianity in Korea: Historical Moments of Protestant Churches*, with selected chapters to share the precious history of Korean churches with our ecumenical friends from around the world who will visit Korea for the WCC 10th Assembly in Busan.

This book is largely divided into two eras, before and after the country's independence from Japanese colonial rule in 1945, because the social status of Protestant churches rapidly changed after independence. Before independence, Protestant churches were not separated from Western culture and society. In this era, Christianity had a great influence on the modernization of Korea as a foreign religion. After independence, Protestant churches became part of the ruling power under the short US military government and the Rhee Syngman government. Churches became an influential social entity and at the same time, one of the major religions in Korea. In this era, churches became diversified based on different faith traditions and theological backgrounds.

Christianity had a great influence on people and society as one of the Korean religions.

The NCCK hopes this book can contribute to revitalizing the spirit of Christianity in Korea and to laying a foundation for churches' common, spiritual future. The NCCK is particularly glad to share the history of Korean Protestant churches in this book with our ecumenical friends around the world.

October 2013
Kim Youngju
General Secretary of the NCCK

CONTENTS

Religion

Nation

After the independence

Education

Woman

Religion

▓ Nation

Christianity in Korea

Before the independence in 1945

Education · Medical Treatment

Woman · Culture

Religion

Nation

Education
· Medical Treatment

Emperor Gojong and Empress Myungsung Grant School
Names

The First Modern Schools,
Baejae and Kyungshin,
and the First Girls' Schools,
Ewha and Chungshin

01 Education

The first modern school in Korea was Baejae
School. This school was opened on August 3, 1885 by Henry G.
Appenzeller, a missionary of the US Northern Methodist Church.
He first arrived in Korea on April 5, 1885 but went to Japan to
escape from the unstable political situation in Korea. He studied
Korean in Japan and came back to Korea on June 21. He then
stayed with William B. Scranton and started to teach English to
two Korean students, Lee Gyumla* and Ko Youngpil, on August
3. This was the beginning of Baejae School. Working through the

* In this book, family names come first for Korean names following the Korean order.

▶ Baejae School

US Legation, Appenzeller officially sought permission from the Korean government to found the school, and he obtained permission for an English school in November. Baejae School officially opened on June 8, 1886.

Few young people applied to Baejae School since they were afraid that attending a Christian school would make them targets of religious persecution. The missionaries made plans to reach out to the Royal Family to build a relationship and to build trust. On January 16, 1887, they had a skating competition on the frozen pond at Deoksu Palace. They demonstrated their skating skills in front of Emperor Gojong and Empress Myungsung, and the Emperor and the Empress granted them special dishes. On February 21, almost one month later, Emperor Gojong granted a special name to the school: Baejae, which means 'a house of educating capable human resources.' The story that the Emperor granted a name to the school founded by missionaries was spread nationwide. Baejae School attracted students from all over the country and was recognized as a good school and a shortcut for success. A new school building was needed with the increase of students, so Appenzeller started building a new school in early 1887. In September, Baejae School had a Renaissance style school building with classrooms, a library and a chapel.

Baejae School had an educational motto written in Chinese characters meaning "a person who wants to be big has to be called by others." This motto originated from the bible passage "Instead whoever wants to become great among you must be your servant"(Mathew 20:26). The East Building of Baejae School still remains in Chung-dong, Seoul. This building built in 1916 is now used as a museum. Behind the East Building there is a 550-year-old Chinese juniper which has a big nail in it. According to legend, a Japanese warrior named Kiyomasa hammered the nail to hang a horse carcass during Imjin War.* The famous poet Kim Soweol, a graduate of Baejae School, loved this tree. There is a small stone monument engraved with "The First Newspaper Office(Sammun Publishing) Site" in front of East Building.

Ewha School was the first modern girls' school in Korea. It was opened by Mary F. Scranton, the mother of William B. Scranton. Mary F. Scranton arrived in Korea on June 20, 1885, one month later than her son. She tried to establish a school but could not find Korean girls who wanted to learn due to the feudalistic social order which disregarded women's education

* This war from 1592–1598 occurred when Japan attacked Korea.

and due to people's cautious attitude toward Westerners. She then bought nineteen old houses on the hill across from the US Legation in Chung-dong and started building a tile-roofed school with more than 200 rooms.

On May 31, 1886, during the construction of the school, a woman named Kim – a concubine of a government official – visited the school and became the first student. She intended to learn English and to work for Empress Myungsung as a translator to help her husband assume a high-level public office. She dropped out of the school, however, after three months of attendance. One day in June, a six-year-old girl named Boksoon visited the school with her mother. Her family was extremely poor and her mother heard that the school would provide food, clothing and education to children free of charge. Her mother wanted the school to take care of Boksoon. The third

▶ Appenzeller and students in the early year at Baejae School

student at Ewha School was Byeoldan, a four-year old girl. She was infected with plague and abandoned together with her mother in the corner of one of the city walls. Mary F. Scranton found them and brought them to the school. In November 1886, the construction of the school and the dormitory was finished. The school gradually established itself as a shelter for poor and marginalized women.

By 1887 the number of students had increased to forty six, and a new teacher, Louisa C. Rothweiler, took a teaching job in October of the same year. In the fall of 1887, Empress Myungsung granted the name 'Ewha' which means 'pear flower' to the school. Pear flower was one of the royal patterns of Yi Dynasty and was a symbol of oriental beauty. Ewha School like Baejae School received acknowledgment by the nation and the public with the acceptance of its name from the Royal Family. More importantly, Korean women began to open their hearts and minds and to acknowledge the educational work of missionaries.

Lee Kyungsook was born in a poor scholar's family in 1851 and became a widow three days after her wedding. She came to meet Mary F. Scranton on the introduction of one of her relatives. She was deeply touched by Scranton's polite manner that was different from many Koreans' disrespect to her. She studied at Ewha School and became the first Korean teacher in April 1889. The site of Ewha School is presently the campus of Ewha High School. The site of the tile-roofed school building is now in the grass field of the school and a bust of Mary F. Scranton is standing at the site. There are other historical remains on the campus, such as a pond where Yoo Kwansoon* did the wash, the site of Hotel Sontag** and parts of old city walls. On the left of the East Gate is Simpson Hall, a classroom building of Ewha School that was built in 1915.

Kyungshin School was opened by Horace G. Underwood, a missionary of the US Northern Presbyterian Church, on May 11, 1886. Underwood first started the school as an orphanage. He was teaching students at Jejungwon*** and made plans to establish an orphanage in January 1886. He envisioned a boarding school that could take care of orphans and children from poor families and provide them with vocational training. He bought a house in Chung-dong on May 11 and renovated it. He then opened a school with one student. The name of the school was Underwood School and then changed to Christian School, Minroa School and Guse School. Eventually the school had its permanent name, Kyungshin School, in 1905, four years after James S. Gale of the US Northern Presbyterian Church was inaugurated as the headmaster in 1901. Kyungshin

---

* She was a graduate of Ewha School and one of leading activists of the independence movement during the Japanese colonial rule. She died in prison at the age of seventeen.

** This was built by a German woman named Sontag in 1902 and one of the first modern hotels in Korea.

*** This was the first modernized hospital, established by US missionary H. N. Allen in 1885 with the support of the Korean government.

▶ Teachers and students at Baejae School in the 1900s

means 'perceiving new knowledge.' Edwin W. Koons was inaugurated as the 8ᵗʰ headmaster and decided the school motto, 'freedom, equality, humanity.'

In April 1915, Kyungshin School could begin providing college level education thanks to the effort of Underwood, the first headmaster. Yonhee College(now Yonsei University) was established two years later as a continuation of this program. In 1938, the Department of Mission of the US Northern Presbyterian Church rejected the Japanese Government-General's coercion to worship at the Japanese shrine and decided to close the school. Then, when graduates, teachers and church leaders made efforts to reopen the school, the Department of Mission resigned from the management of the school. Kim Hongryang and Kim Wonryang, Christian brothers from Anak in Hwanghae-do took over the school, and Choi Taeyoung was inaugurated as the first Korean headmaster. In

April 1940, the school moved to Jungneung and was destroyed by a fire in 1952. The school moved again to Haehwa-dong in 1957 and remains there still today.

In the house in Chung-dong where Horace N. Allen was living, three women were also living together: Ellers A. Bunker(later Mrs. Banger), a nurse, Lillas S. Horton(later Mrs. Underwood) and Mary E. Hayden(later Mrs. Giford). Chungshin Girls' School began here. In June 1887, Bunker brought a five-year old girl named Jungne and started teaching her. This was the beginning of the school.

In October 1895, Chungdong Girls' School had a new building in Yeonji-dong, Jongno-gu and changed its name to Yeondong Girls' School and again to Chungshin Girls' School on August 11, 1909. In 1906, the school constructed a two-storied Western style building on the hill behind Yeondong Church for classrooms and a dormitory, and a new three-storied Renaissance style building in 1910. This building was constructed thanks to a donation from L. H. Severance and therefore was called the Severance Building. It was the most modernized building in Seoul in terms of its size and facilities. This building still remains. In 1904, Emperor Gojong moved into the first building of Chungdong Girls' School and the building obtained a new name, Jungmyungjeong which means 'a palace with constant light.'

Hyupsung, Pyongyang, and Kyungsung Theological Schools Open

The work of missionaries in Korea had three components: schools, hospitals and churches. Missionaries taught Korean Christians about the bible and Christian doctrines, and then made them church leaders. The beginning of Korean theological schools was the intensive bible and doctrinal education at churches and mission schools.

Henry C. Appenzeller from the US Northern Methodist Church established Baejae School in Chung-dong(1885) and wanted to run English literature, Chinese literature and theology courses. He could easily start English literature and

Chinese literature courses but could not publicly have the theology course. However, two students, Han Youngkyung and Park Jungsang came to learn the bible and Christian doctrines. Appenzeller educated and baptized them.

In September 1887, Appenzeller bought a traditional Korean house to use for theological courses. This house was not far from Baejae School and he named it Bethel Church. He found eight students in Baejae School who were eager to learn the bible and started to educate them. The 1887 annual report of the Department of Mission of the US Northern Methodist Church recognized this as the foundation of the Methodist Theological School in Korea. This was not a well-organized theological school but it was the first theological education program in Korea.

In April 1888, mission activities and religious gatherings were forbidden because of the Myungdong Cathederal construction and baby scandals.* In the 1890s the need to educate Korean christians and church leaders was recognized. The Department of Korean Mission of the US Northern Methodist Church began to run courses to train ministers and this was the beginning of formal theological courses. Though they called it

---

* The Korean government was uncomfortable with the construction plans for Myungdong Cathedral that had the cathedral on city's upper hill from where people could look down the Royal palace. This became one of reasons for the government to forbid Christianity. This scandal was followed by a baby scandal based on horrific rumors that Western missionaries abducted babies and killed them for eating and medical use.

'theological gathering,' theological education was getting more organized.

The theological courses did not have any designated faculty members or independent classrooms. They were more like short-term intensive courses, and missionaries travelled to cities such as Seoul, Pyongyang and Incheon, and they taught theology to Korean mission workers during the off-season in the countryside. Three mission workers who studied in this program, Kim Changsik, Kim Gibeom and Choi Byungheon, passed the preliminary test and were ordained in May 1901 and the following year. The number of Christians increased after the Wonsan Mission Campaign in 1903 and more people were interested in becoming ministers. There was a need to establish a formal theological school.

In 1902 Appenzeller died from an accident at

▶ Missionary Jones and students of 'Theological Gathering' (1896-1900)

▶ Methodist Theological Seminary in early years

sea and theological education faced a big crisis. George H. Jones had been teaching at the Theological Gathering since the 1890s, and he took over Appenzeller's work. He operated the Theological Gathering after the death of Appenzeller and made serious efforts to establish a theological school. As a result, the two mission departments of the US Northern Methodist Church and the Southern Methodist Church established together Hyupsung Biblical Institute(Union Biblical Institute in English) in 1907 and Jones was inaugurated as the first director. This institute provided a five-year theological education program comprised of two semesters each year. It had its own school building at 31 Naengchun-dong and changed its name to Union Methodist Theological Seminary.

In February 1908, Woman's Biblical Institute began in a house in Insa-dong, Jongno-gu, Seoul to train female mission workers. This institute had its own three-storied building by the spring of 1917. For the theological education of women, the two departments of women's mission of the US Northern Methodist Church and Southern Methodist Church agreed to run jointly a women's theological seminary in 1921, and they changed Woman's Biblical Institute to Union Woman's Bible Training School. In December 1931, this school and Union Biblical Institute were integrated and became Methodist Theological Seminary.

Underwood opened a theological course in 1890 and taught the bible to sixteen students. The Department of Mission of the US Presbyterian Church made a rule saying 'any missionary must have a biblical course and teach the bible in his mission field' in 1891. This became the foundation of bible studies in Korea, and the education of a few people selected by missionaries led to the beginning of theological seminaries.

In 1893, the United Association of Missionaries which included missionaries from the US Northern Presbyterian

▶ Methodist Theological Seminary

Church, the Southern Presbyterian Church, the Presbyterian Church of Australia and the Presbyterian Church in Canada, recognized a need for the establishment of a theological seminary and for the support of Koreans in building independent churches to accommodate increasing numbers of Christians and to put into practice the Nevius methods of missions.* The theological course opened by Underwood was followed by the Department of Pyongyang Mission in the late 1890s. Education programs became more active thanks to the effort of missionaries such as Samuel A. Moffett, William M. Baird, William L. Swallen and Graham Lee who had been trained at McCormick Theological Seminary. In 1900, Moffett made detailed plans for a theological school and sent a letter to the US Northern Presbyterian Church sharing the need for a theological school in Korea and requesting funds.

Moffett obtained permission to establish a theological seminary and to take over the responsibility for the establishment from the Department of Mission in 1901. He selected two volunteers, Bang Gichang and Kim Jongseop, from the bible study class and started a theological training program for them. The United Association of Missionaries officially opened a theological seminary of Presbyterian Church of Korea in Pyongyang in January 1902 and selected four students, Yang Jeonbaek, Gil Seonju, Lee Gipoong, and Song Inseo. Two other men, Seo Kyungjo and Han Seokjin who had participated in

---

* These were suggested by John L. Nevius who was then working as a missionary in China.

private training by missionaries were transferred to the seminary in the third year. They became the first ordained pastors of Presbyterian churches in Korea.

The Presbyterian theological seminary closed in 1938 during the Japanese colonial rule because of its rejection of worshiping at the Japanese shrine. This seminary, however, provided a foundation for other seminaries. The Theological Seminary of the Presbyterian Church of Korea and Chongshin University were established based on this foundation. Chosun Seminary(now Hanshin University) opened at Soongdong Church in Seoul in 1940.

The Union Biblical Institute of the Methodist church was in Seoul and progressive, and the Pyongyang Seminary of the Presbyterian church was in Pyongyang and conservative. The former focused more on academic theological education and the latter was more inclined to practical training helpful for pastoral care. This was one of the reasons that there were more theologians from Methodist churches in the early years of the Korean churches. These different theological and educational approaches of different denominations were one of the causes of conflict in the Korean church.

Holiness churches began with Oriental Missionary Society's missions in Korea in 1907. Oriental Missionary Society was established by Charles E. Cowman and Earnest A. Kilbourne and they opened the Tokyo Biblical

Institute. Kim Sangjoon and Jung Bin studied at Tokyo Biblical Institute and encountered Oriental Missionary Society in Tokyo. They returned to Korea after graduation and opened an Oriental Missionary Society biblical mission house in Jongno, Seoul. They started their mission activities and opened a bible study class. They also made plans for a biblical institute. They eventually opened Kyungsung Biblical Institute in Mookyo-dong on March 13, 1911 and John Thomas was inaugurated as the first director. This institute changed its name to Kyungsung Seminary in 1940 and ordained pastor Lee Myungjik assumed the office of dean. After Korea's independence from Japanese colonial rule this seminary changed again to Seoul Seminary which is now Seoul Theological University. Kyungsung Biblical Institute was also the root of Sungkyeol(which means holiness in English) University.

Salvation Army opened Salvation Army Biblical College in Pyung-dong, Jongno-gu, Seoul in February 1910 and changed its name to Salvation Army Officer Training College in 1912.

Anglican churches opened St. Michael Seminary in Gangwha-do(an island in Incheon) on May 10, 1953 and later changed its name to Chunshin Seminary. This became Anglican Theological Seminary and is now Sungkonghoe(meaning Anglican) University.

The Assemblies of God opened Full Gospel Seminary on May 10, 1953 and Arthur Chesnut was inaugurated as the first dean. This seminary changed to Full Gospel Theological Seminary and Soonshin University, and is now Hansei University.

From Children to the Elderly
The Beginning of Sunday Schools

03 Education

Sunday schools first appeared in the church history in the eighteenth century in England during the Industrial Revolution. At that time, children had to work long hours in newly developed factories and could not have any opportunity for education or moral training. They were often ill and even sent to prison. The Sunday school movement began in this social environment. John Wesley's evangelical work and Robert Raikes's Sunday school movement were prominent in English society and had a big influence on other countries as well.

▶ Underwood speaks in front of Sunday School Gathering in 1913

In January 1888, Mary F. Scranton from the US Northern Methodist Church began the first Sunday school in Korea. Twelve female students, three older women and four female missionaries gathered at Ewha School. In March 1888, Henry G. Appenzeller started an English Sunday school at Baejae Church with fourteen students from Baejae School. Mattie W. Noble of the US Northern Methodist Church made an especially big contribution to the Sunday school movement. She was a Sunday school educator and travelled with her husband, William A. Noble. She contributed greatly to establishing Sunday schools in churches in Pyongyang, Youngbyeon, Haeju, Kyungsung, Jinnampo, Suwon and Incheon.

In October 1892, Mattie Noble organized a Sunday school for youth. She also started Sunday schools for women and children in Ahyun Church in September 1893. This was the first children's Sunday school. The Sunday schools begun by Scranton and Appenzeller were for the students from Ewha and Baejae Schools and not for children. In 1897, five Sunday schools were begun in Pyongyang and printed texts were used from 1898. In 1905, the Federal Council of Missions was organized and Presbyterian and Methodist churches jointly edited and published Sunday school textbooks.

Mattie Noble started training Sunday school teachers in Namsanhyun Church in Pyongyang and established a Sunday school for children in 1903. There were 200 children from the age of five to fifteen and more than twenty teachers. In April 1911, a Sunday school for infants was begun and 115 infants were registered that year. The Sunday school in Namsanhyun Church was the first to use common texts and the first to separate classes according to children's ages and education levels.

The Sunday school of the Presbyterian Church of Korea began in Yeondong Church on May 5, 1907. This Sunday school had more than 900 children in 1914 when adult members numbered about 700.

In September 1893, the mission department of the Methodist Church organized the Sunday School Association to publish bible study books and Sunday school textbooks in demand by churches. The association of Methodist Sunday schools was organized to exchange information, publish textbooks and strengthen cooperation among Sunday schools.

In 1905, the Korea Protestant Council for Missions organized a Sunday school committee with the participation of eight missionaries including William N. Blair and Mattie Noble. Koreans participated in this committee beginning in 1911. They were Hyun Soon, Yoon Chiho, Han Seokwon and Hong Byungseon from the Methodist church and Namgung Hyuk from the Presbyterian church. In April 1911, Frank L. Brown who was then in charge of the Asia Desk of the World Sunday School Association visited Korea. This became a good opportunity for Korean churches to expand the Sunday school association. This association was the origin of the Korea Christian Education Association. The Sunday school committee published bible study textbooks for the Sunday schools. Yoon Chiho first participated in the fifth World Sunday School Convention held in Rome in May 1907 and made a speech. He was elected as a member of the standing committee. Yoon Chiho, Rhee Syngman and Shin Heungwoo participated afterward in the world convention as Korean representatives and represented Korea's Sunday school movement.

In November 2-9, 1921, the first National Sunday School Gathering took place at the YMCA and Taewhagwan in Seoul. More than 1,300 people from all over the country participated in the gathering. As a result of this gathering the Chosun Sunday School Association was organized. Han Seokwon, the general secretary of this association, contributed to the spread of summer Sunday schools. In 1922, Chungdong First Methodist Church had a summer Sunday school with five teachers and about 100 children participating. This was the beginning of children's summer Sunday school in Korea. The national Sunday school gathering took place every four years. The second gathering was held in Seoul in 1925, the third in Pyongyang in 1929 and the fourth in Daegu in 1933. These gatherings contributed to the education of Sunday school teachers and the growth of churches.

In the Sunday school gatherings people would perform folk musical and sing Dansimga* to encourage the solidarity of Koreans from all thirteen provinces and the national spirit to resist Japan. In January 1925, a Sunday school magazine was first published. On March 1, 1926, a Christian children's magazine, *Children's Life*, was published but it was discontinued due to Japanese oppression on April 1, 1944. The first children's magazine in Korea was published by Methodist pastor Han Seokwon in December 1920. Christians also played a leading role in encouraging children's welfare through publishing magazines.

When the third Sunday school gathering took place in Pyongyang, participants started a campaign to increase Sunday schools. The campaign continued for the next four years and this was the beginning of the Christian education campaign. In January 1930, *Religious Education Monthly*(now *Christian*

---

* This is a traditional song composed by Chung Mongju who lived in the late fourteenth century. He showed his patriotism for the declining country by singing this song.

Education) was published. August 29 was observed as the Sunday School Sunday(now Christian Education Sunday) in 1933.

Methodist churches were not happy with the Chosun Sunday School Association that was led by Presbyterian churches and eventually established the Methodist Religious Education Association in 1928. This organization became the Education Department of the Korean Methodist Church in 1930 and Methodist churches developed their own church education system. In 1934, Presbyterian churches established the Education Department and published their own Sunday school textbooks. In these changes the role of the Chosun Sunday School Association gradually weakened. It had an extraordinary general meeting on June 21, 1938 and suspended its activities due to Japan's oppression. On January 14, 1947, it had a reconstruction general meeting and resumed its activities, overcoming the pain of the past and the conflict among churches. It was an association of Methodist and Presbyterian churches before and now the new organization included membership of Baptist churches.

In 1948, the name of organization changed from the Chosun Sunday School Association to the Korea Council of Christian Education. The organization's work also changed from focusing on Sunday schools for children to educating youth and adults members as well. It also expanded its boundaries of Christian education from education in Sunday schools and churches to education in families, schools and society.

In 1956 after two years of discussion and editing, all members from Methodist, Presbyterian and Baptist churches agreed upon common Sunday school textbooks. In 1959, the Presbyterian Church in the Republic of Korea obtained membership, adding one more member to the organization. In 1959, the first national Christian education meeting was held and has continued to take place every two to four years. Since 1960 it has also hosted annual training programs for Sunday school teachers, especially for summer Sunday schools.

The Sunday school movement in Korea played a very important role in teaching church members the bible and Christian doctrines. This education was not limited to children but expanded to teens, young adults and the elderly. As a result, it greatly contributed to churches' growth. But Sunday schools in Korea are facing many challenges and difficulties now. It is the time to develop a new paradigm considering that churches in Korea began and grew because of the Sunday schools.

Missionaries Train Medical Workers before the Government's Program

The Beginning of Korean Nursing Education

04 Medical Treatment

Western medical practice was directly imported to Korea after the Gangwhado Agreement in 1876 and Western hospitals were established. Koreans had unprofessional supporting jobs of administration, pharmacy and nursing during the early days of Western hospitals. When hospitals were getting bigger, Koreans started taking over professional duties. In 1903, Bogu Hospital began the first nursing training and Severance, Dongin, Daehan and other private hospitals followed them in providing formal nursing trainings. Four nurses finished the formal training by 1910.

Jejung, the first Western hospital, did not even have a clear understanding of nursing as a professional job. Horace G. Underwood worked as a nurse immediately after the opening of Jejung Hospital. He did not have any formal training. However, he was a talented nurse with a 'soft, gentle, quiet, prepared, skillful and humble' attitude. He was recognized as a good nurse with a caring mind.

Jejung soon needed female medical staff because Korean society was strict and did not allow direct physical contact between men and women. The hospital needed people who could freely work with both men and women, so with advice from Korean friends Horace N. Allen tried to solve this problem by recruiting prostitutes. Prostitutes were the only women who could have physical contact with men and be exempt from the social norms forbidding the direct contact between men and women. Allen presented this idea to the Korean government which then sent out official recruiting letters to Hwanghae-do and Pyongan-do and asked them to select girls from among their official prostitutes. These two local governments sent five girls to Seoul who became medical students on August 5, 1885. Allen assigned them to nursing and pharmaceutical jobs. However, two of them were blamed for making trouble in the hospital and were fired at Allen's request and the other three of them were sold to a Chinese general, Won Se Gye. The activity of female medical staff ended in four months.

In 1895, cholera epidemic was widespread and

the Korean government made plans to establish quarantine stations and hospitals in Uiju, Incheon and Pyongyang. At this time the term "nursing" began taking root in Korean society, although the public understanding of nursing was still limited to the undertaking of unimportant minor duties and it was considered a men's job. Only in 1907 did the Korean government begin modern nursing education. In this year the government established Daehan Hospital and set up a system to train nurses and midwives. But this kind of nursing training had already been started by missionaries who understood the need for nursing staff even before the government's decision.

Modern nursing education in Korea began with the establishment of a three-year nursing school at Bogu Hospital by Margaret J. Edmunds in 1903. At this time the term "nurse"(ganhowon in Korean) was first used. This word used Chinese characters and was coined by missionaries who were looking for an appropriate word for professional women who took care of patients. However, the school had difficulties to find students because nursing jobs were not familiar to the public and there was almost no job training for women other than prostitutes in Korean society.

Eventually, six women who had worked at hospitals and pharmacies applied to the school. These students paid tuition every year and the school provided them with boarding fees, laundry service, nursing uniforms and books. They could sign a contract after finishing a two-month training program and they worked regular hospital hours wearing a nursing uniform. This uniform was designed by mixing Korean and Western patterns with consideration for the active work of nurses. It was the first nurse uniform in Korea.

In the first year, the students took classes of qualities of good nursing, skeletal structure, circulatory system, blood tests, hospital regulations, making poultices, bedding, bed making, ventilation, operation preparation and historical figures. In the second year, they learned emergency measures, dentistry, dietetic treatment, gynecology, anatomy and Nightingale's life. In the last year, classes related to sanitation, antipyresis, operation and surgical treatment were provided. In the early years of the school the daily curriculum was basically comprised of twelve hours of work, including both class work and a practicum. In the later years, detailed nursing practice courses such as bandaging, bed making, bathing, medication, simple cooking for dietetic treatment and vital sign testing were added. Students could take classes of the bible, music, mathematics, Korean, Chinese and English in addition to nursing classes. But the facilities of Bogu Hospital were rather poor for practice. The school therefore sent two students to Nagasaki Hospital in Japan in 1905 so that they could have more practical experience and visit other hospitals.

Two of the six students, Maria Kim and Grace Lee, completed the training program and were given nurse hats at a ceremony held in the lobby of Bogu Hospital on January 25, 1906. It was the first commencement ceremony for trained nurses. The lobby was decorated with Korean and US flags, and many women from both countries participated in the ceremony. Edmunds granted nurse hats to the two graduates and the medical staff of the hospital congratulated them on completing the professional education with songs and prayers. The two graduates' training continued for next two years and the final commencement ceremony was held on November 5, 1908. The second ceremony was held in Chungdong Church for the students who had studied in training schools at Bogu Hospital and Severance Hospital in 1907. At that time, granting hats was understood as a ceremony for men entering adulthood in Korea, so the ceremony granting official hats to women caught attention from the general public.

It was September 1906 when Severance Hospital established a nurse training school. Esther L. Shields who was then in charge of nursing work in Severance Hospital and Margaret J. Edmunds of Bogu Hospital had a discussion about establishing a joint nursing training school so that the nursing staff in the two hospitals could develop professional skills and have more practical experiences. They agreed to run the school separately but to have joint classes and practices. But their plan was not realized. In 1909, the nurse training school of Severance Hospital educated students from the two schools and provided them with eight classes of anatomy, vital sign testing, dietetic treatment, ophthalmology, internal medicine, mass measurement, microbiology and nursing practice. The first commencement ceremony of Severance Hospital's school was held

▶ Nursing staff at Severance Hospital

in June 12, 1910 and one student, Kim Baese was granted the nursing hat.

In early years, nurses could not tend to male patients due to strict social conditions. Then there was a historical landmark. On August 1, 1907, Japan discharged Korean soldiers to integrate Korea officially into Japan. Korean soldiers strongly resisted and fought back in downtown areas. In this battle many soldiers were wounded and nurses had to tend to male patients for the first time. It was a tragic moment of Korea's history and at the same time, a moment of birth for professional nurses in Korean society. Oliver R. Avison recalled the moment as follows.

"Korean nurses were very reluctant to tend to male patients. Young female nurses did not have any experience of taking care of male patients. They just looked at many wounded soldiers lying down. Then they realized that the

soldiers got wounded to fight for them and the nation, and they had a responsibility to take care of the soldiers. One of the nurses stepped forward breaking old social norms and started tending to wounded soldiers. All other nurses followed her⋯ Korean nurses worked overnight and all day in the next day. They then realized that they were tending to male patients. They thought that they already broke social norms and could take care of male patients again⋯the soldiers leaving the battle ground were in tears and the nurses watching the soldiers burst into tears as well⋯after this event male patients in my hospital could have more qualified care service. It could have been difficult to provide good care service if only male nurses had continued tending to male patients. But female nurses eventually began taking care of male patients."

Devotion to the Eradication of Tuberculosis

Christmas Seals and Sherwood Hall

05 Medical Treatment

Christmas seals were first designed to raise funds for TB(tuberculosis) patients and were therefore called 'TB Christmas seals.' Sherwood Hall, a medical missionary from the US Northern Methodist Church first designed and printed Christmas seals in Korea. He worked in Korea as a medical missionary, following in the footsteps of his parents, William J. Hall and Rosetta S. Hall. In particular, he studied TB and devoted his life to Korean TB patients. On October 27, 1928, he established the first modern nursing home in Korea for TB patients.

He designed Christmas seals in 1931 while he was staying in the US for sabbatical. He learned about Christmas seals from Emily P. Bissell who was the chair of the US TB Association. In 1932, he returned to Korea and worked on Christmas seals. First he obtained permission from the Japanese Government-General. In 1933, he printed the first edition of Christmas seals with a picture of two sisters in Hanbok(Korean traditional costume) with a pine tree behind them. He was able to raise 350 won in funds from the first edition of Christmas seals. The funds were sent to the hospitals that were treating TB patients: fifty won to Christian Hospital in Pyongyang, fifty won to St. Anna Hospital in Yeoju, fifty won to Jehye Hospital in Hamheung, seventy five won to Severance Hospital in Seoul and seventy five won to Guse Nursing Home in Haeju. Fifty won was allocated for publicity and research. The number of TB patients in

▶ Christmas seal in 1936

Korea gradually decreased because the fundraising with Christmas seals continued and all the profit from Christmas seals was used for TB patients.

Sherwood Hall was born in Seoul on November 10, 1893. His father, William Hall worked in Pyongyang as a missionary and died from typhus on November 24, 1884. Sherwood Hall was one-year old then and his mother, Rosetta Hall was pregnant. She returned to the US with her son and two Koreans, Park Esther and Park Yoosan accompanied her. Park Esther later became the first female Korean medical doctor. In 1897, Rosetta Hall visited Korea again with her four-year old son, Sherwood and three-year old daughter, Edith. Park Esther and Park Yoosan did not accompany them this time and stayed in the US for Park Esther's medical study. Rosetta Hall stayed in Seoul for a while then went to Pyongyang where her husband had worked. Edith died from dysentery immediately after her arrival in Pyongyang on May 23, 1898. Sherwood Hall became one of the first students of the international school in Pyongyang in 1900. He studied there until 1908 and moved to Mount Vermont School in Massachusetts in 1911. He graduated from this school in 1915. He entered the University of Mount Union in Ohio and graduated from this school in 1919. He then moved to Canada and studied at Toronto Medical School. He finished his studies in 1923. On April 19, 1926, he went to Korea again to work as a missionary and inherited his parents' legacy.

There was a story that made Sherwood Hall especially interested in TB. This story was related to Park Esther and Park Yoosan who accompanied him and his mother when they returned to the US. Park Esther studied medicine in the US and her husband worked hard and supported his wife for six years. But Park Yoosan died from TB on April 28, 1900 when Park Esther was graduating and expecting to return to Korea. Park Esther buried him in Baltimore and returned to Korea alone. Park Esther was the first Korean medical doctor and helped with Rosetta Hall's medical treatment. She treated more than 3,000 patients in ten months. She was also in charge of Bogu Hospital and opened a new era in which Korean female doctors could treat Korean women. Sherwood Hall and his family liked her a lot. Park Esther got sick after ten years of hard work and devotion to her patients. She suffered from TB like her husband did. On April 13, 1910 her short life ended at the age of thirty four. Sherwood Hall was seventeen at that time and he was shocked by her death.

"Esther's death was a shocking event to me. She was in the golden years of her life but suddenly fell sick. TB took away her life and the lives of many other people whom she loved very much. I made up my mind to devote myself to eradicating TB. I decided to be a medical expert in TB and to come back to Korea. I also decided to build a nursing facility for TB patients in Korea. I recalled several times what Dr. Heidi had told me and I had stored deeply in my mind. Noble ideals and motivations cannot be realized without spiritual power."

In November 1984, Sherwood Hall and his wife Marian Hall visited Korea at the invitation of the Korean National Tuberculosis Association. He was eighty eight and was pleased to come to Korea since he missed it very much. In fact, the association did not know about Sherwood Hall even though there was a photo of him on the wall of the organization's entrance. They did not know whether he was alive or whether he was English, Canadian or American. Then his memoir 'Dr. Hall's memories of Chosun' was translated into Korean and published. The association eventually came to know about Sherwood Hall and invited him and his wife to Korea. Sherwood Hall was very pleased to visit the country where he had been born and to which he had devoted his life. He lived a very humble and simple life and could not even find a good suit to wear for his visit to Korea. He had not had a suit for decades. His friends gathered some money and bought him a suit. His wife decided to borrow some clothes from friends. They sent her clothes when they heard her story.

On April 5, 1991, Sherwood Hall died at the age of ninety nine. He was buried in Yangwhajin Foreign Missionary Cemetery in Seoul where his parents and little sister had been buried. His wife, Marian Hall died five months later. She was also buried with the Sherwood family.

Woman · Culture

Revolutionary Idea in the Seventh Commandment

Stop Concubinage!

In 1906, *Family Magazine* published by Sandong Youth School of Sangdong Church had an article which wrote as follows.

"···*this country misunderstands women and also misunderstands natural laws. Are there any bad practices in society and families caused by disrespecting women? There are many, and first of all, we have to talk about the evil practices relating to women. It is not easy to talk about all of them as they are rooted in the bad custom that respects men and disrespects women. In particular, a few evil practices are worse than others.*

The first evil custom is having concubines. At the beginning of the universe there were sky, land and all creatures. Among them human beings were created with a divine spirit. It is based on the natural laws that a man and a woman become a couple. It is appropriate that all the people in the world find a man or woman to be a couple. It is not right for a woman to have two husbands and for a man to have two wives. However in this country there is a bad custom that disrespects women. Because of this custom, it is a big scandal if a woman has two or three husbands and a widow cannot even remarry. But a married man usually has concubines and some men even have seven or eight concubines. There are few men who do not have concubines and they are regarded as neither masculine nor capable. There are many people who destroy families due to their evil practice of having concubines. There are many families that have conflict and eventually come apart. Concubines' children are discriminated against due to a bad custom that treats children of wives and concubines differently. How can we deal with these problems? …"

This article first pointed out the evil practice of having concubines and three additional problems in following paragraphs. It pointed out an evil practice of not teaching women. The reason was because women were not regarded as human beings, it said. And it also pointed out a bad custom that favored male children and disrespected women.

This custom originated from wrong Confucian teachings that had been part of Korean social life since the foundation of Yi Dynasty. Confucianism was only used as a means to control people. This wrong custom was taught and learned for a long time and settled down in society as a means for women to oppress women as well as for men to control women. In fact, in upper class families it was regarded as natural for men to have concubines and it was sometimes used as a criterion to appreciate men's ability. This custom of concubinage was an evil practice that made both wives and concubines stuck in an unhappy situation. As an example, Jeon Samdeok, a famous mission worker lived a very difficult and lonely life due to her husband's relationship with a concubine. She accepted the bible and lived a new life devoting to spreading the bible.

Concubinage was understood as a custom and was not regarded as a problem to fix. Even the intellectuals who led modern reform movements in 1884 and 1894 neither paid attention to this problem nor included any clauses about it in their declarations. The declaration of Gapo Reform in 1894 included a clause saying 'an adopted son is allowed only when the wife and concubines do not have any sons.' This clause in fact acknowledged concubinage. In 1915, the Japanese Government-General forbade the registration of concubines as family members and monogamy became a legal requirement.

In the late nineteenth century, people's understanding of concubinage changed with the introduction of

Christianity. There was a big influence of missionaries from the US who were the majority in charge of Korean missions. They emphasized Western human ethics and especially monogamy. They understood a practice against monogamy as breaking the seventh commandment and considered monogamy a semi-doctrine. This was a revolutionary action and provided Korean society with a foundation to reform attitudes towards family and women, and also provided Christians with an opportunity to enhance their Christian ethics. In 1907, a repentance movement began in Pyongyang and the most serious sin many people repented was concubinage and adultery.

Churches regarded conbubinage as a sin and people having concubines could not come to the church. Some people were kicked out of the church when their relationships with concubines were revealed. In 1910, Saemoonan Church excommunicated No Byungsang due to his relationship with a concubine and punished Yoo Hojoon for six months. Yoo had brought a woman who had abandoned her husband to his house and slept with her. Hong Jongik of Namyang Church was ashamed of his behavior of having a concubine and sent the concubine back home.

In Gaksimsa Church, a branch church of Dongdaemoon Church, a similar happening was witnessed in 1910. Gaksimsa village was famous for shamans. In this village men usually had one or two concubines. Rev. Kim Jongwoo who was sent to Gaksimsa prayed and seriously recommended people to stop concubinage. Thanks to his prayer and persuasion many people stopped concubinage and devoted their hearts and minds to Christ. Among these people, there was a man named Song Sinmook.

"Song Sinmook was an influential gentleman in the village. He had two concubines. I and fellow Christians recommended him many times to send his concubines back home. But he did not have courage. Then one day I prayed with him and recommended him again with many words. He eventually wept with pain and repented his sin. He sent his concubines back home and decided to devote his heart and mind to Christ's work. He has been working hard as a child of Lord until now. With Song Sinmook's repentance all members of Gaksimsa Church could enjoy the grace of God. In addition, two churches were established in Joonggyeri and Changdong near to Gaksimsa. Three mission workers were trained in Gaksimsa and all of them have been devoted to Christ's work."

Song Sinmook became a mission worker and devoted his life to missions in Gaksimsa Church.

Koreans' Gateways to Christianity
Anti-Christian Actions

Protestantism was introduced to Korea in 1884 and missionaries could begin missions in a relatively advantageous environment due to Emperor Gojong's permission of Christian missions. But this did not mean that mission activities in the early years were all smooth. In the late Yi Dynasty,* there were small and big persecutions resulting from entangled religious and political issues such as continuous persecutions of Catholics, academic controversies and

---

* This is the last kingdom of Korea and missionaries came to Korea in the declining era of this kingdom.

confrontations over orthodox Confucianism, newly introduced academic traditions that were the foundation of the persecution, pro-US intellectuals' increasing power, expanding US missionaries' activities and the anti-opening intellectuals' sense of crisis.

In particular, when Protestantism first came to Korea people could not differentiate Protestantism from Catholicism. People would understand all missionaries as evil people who were spreading evil knowledge. People would call all Western religions Catholicism and be an enemy to it. But the Korean government signed on agreements with Asian and Western countries and the political situation changed when Protestantism was introduced. There was no bloody persecution, unlike the series of persecutions of Catholics in earlier years. In spite of this changed situation, missionaries had to face unexpected difficulties in mission trips. They were very often not allowed to stay in public accommodations and stoned and abused verbally.

In this environment, a few big persecutions of Christians happened. The first event was an anti-Christian campaign that was called the 'baby scandal' and happened in 1888. This sandal was begun with the rumors that Christian schools, orphanages and hospitals abducted babies and cut out their eyes for medical experiments. People were upset and attacked churches, foreign residents, schools and hospitals. This event was similar to one that had happened in Chunjin, China in

1870. The event in China also began with similar rumors and became an anti-Christian campaign. As a result, a number of missionaries, workers of foreign legations and Christians were killed in China.

It was presumed that anti-opening politicians who felt a sense of crisis due to the pro-US intellectuals' increasing power spread the rumors. The rumors were very similar to the rumors found in Chunjin, China when there was a big anti-Christian campaign. It was therefore not difficult to imagine that those intellectuals who sought political interests in Korea imitated the rumors and campaign in China. People were easily exposed to the rumors and became enraged. They attacked Christian schools and hospitals. Ewha School in Chung-dong was seriously damaged and foreign legations ordered missionaries not to go out of their residences.

The second was the Doryook Secret Order Scandal. One day in November 1900, a secret letter from Emperor Gogjong arrived at local Confucian shrines all over the country. The letter delivering Emperor's order was signed by Lee Yongik and Kim Youngjoon who were pro-Russian high-ranking officials. The Emperor ordered in the letter to "slaughter all missionaries and Christians on December 6(October 15 according to the lunar calendar) all over the country." Underwood, a US missionary, was travelling in Hwanghae-do at that time and obtained this letter with the help of a supporter on November 20. He immediately sent a telegraph to his office in Seoul.

Underwood thought that telegraph operators or government officials could snatch his telegraph away and abolish it. He decided to send the telegraph not in English or Korean that Koreans could read but in Latin that only missionaries could understand. The mission department of the US Presbyterian Church went to the US Legation immediately after getting the telegraph. Allen who was then the US minister to Korea went to the Royal Palace with the telegraph and met Emperor Gojong and Park Jaesoon, the Minister of Foreign Affairs to ask about the secret letter. In fact, Emperor Gojong did not send any secret letter and Lee Yongik and Kim Youngjoon did not sign on such a fake letter either. Both of them appealed their innocence. A few days later, the Korean government sent a letter to local governments. This letter emphasized that the previous secret letter was counterfeit and ordered to be prepared for unexpected incidents attacking Christians. Big persecutions were prevented thanks to the effort of the government and foreign officials. But small incidents constantly happened in villages and Christians were beaten and arrested throughout the winter of 1900.

This scandal was influenced by the Uihwadan incident that had happened and frightened people in the summer of the same year in China. This was a massive anti-Christian campaign spread in Shandong and Shanxi, China from 1899 to the summer of 1900. 230 missionaries and 40,000 Christians were killed due to this campaign. Many missionaries and Chinese Christians escaped to Korea. Eight Western countries organized allied forces to protect their citizens and fought with the Chinese government that supported Uihwadan militants. The Chinese government lost this war and gradually declined afterward.

In the summer of 1900, an anti-Christian campaign that imitated the Uihwadan incident in China and led by people affiliated with Donghak* and Hwalbindang** emerged in Korea. Missionaries and Christians were beaten, churches were destroyed and Christian families' houses were set on fire all over the country that summer. Western newspapers reported that Uihwadan's anti-Christian campaign was also happening in Korea. It was in this situation that the secret letter was delivered to local shrines and missionaries thought with fear that their concerns had become reality. They pointed out Donghak and Hwalbindang as the forces behind the scandal. The 'baby scandal' was an anti-Christian campaign led by anti-opening conservative intellectuals and the secret letter scandal was led by the general public. But like the activities of other organized groups, the anti-Christian campaign by Donghak and Hwalbindang declined after Korea lost its sovereignty due to Japan's occupation. Anti-Japan movements replaced the campaign against Christianity at this time.

In the 1920s, there was another anti-Christian

---

* This is a Korean indigenous religion founded in 1860.

** This is an anti-imperialistic and anti-feudalistic military group that was active from 1900 to 1904.

campaign led by socialists. In the early 1920s, socialism was introduced to Korea as a new ideological trend. Socialism asserted anti-religious slogans in its early years in terms of ideological and theoretical approaches. In 1925, socialists showed their anti-Christian attitude in a public campaign. They tried to disturb the Second Korea Sunday School Gathering with 3,000 participants from October 21 to 28, 1925. The socialist group Hanyang Youth Association made a plan to organize anti-Christian gatherings and lectures in Insa-dong on October 25 and 26. This plan was targeting the Sunday school gathering organized by Presbyterian and Methodist churches. Some Christians who were already in Seoul for the gathering found the advertising panel of the socialist group. They were very upset and strongly protested against the gathering. Then the police came and ordered the removal of the advertising panel. The anti-Christian gatherings of socialists were banned by the Japanese police. But there was a suspicious rumor after this event that Christians were in a close relationship with Japan and this suspicion was abused for anti-Christian campaigns.

On December 25, 1925, Shinheung Youth Association organized an anti-Christian gathering to disturb Christmas and in January 1926, Hanyang Youth Association decided to observe anti-Christian day on Christmas. From late 1925 to early 1926 socialist youth groups all over the country organized gatherings and lectures to criticize Christianity. They also considered mission workers like Kim Ikdu to be encouraging superstition and called them "high-ranking shamans." They would disturb mission gatherings. But in November 1926, the socialist movement changed its position from focusing on classism to cooperating with nationalists. As a result, socialists considered Christians as a nationalistic group and their anti-Christian campaigns ended. Nationalist Christians like Park Dongwan and Yoo Ikjeom participated in the discussion on organizing a national cooperative front. In February 1927, Shinganhoe, a nationalistic group was established and Lee Sangjae, the former secretary general of the YMCA, assumed the office of chair. Socialists' anti-Christian campaigns were officially over.

The anti-Christian campaigns in the last years of Yi Dynasty emerged when Christianity was not recognized as one of the Korean religions. But the anti-Christian sentiment gradually diminished in the late 1920s as Christians actively participated in nationalistic movements. Christianity lived with Koreans and was recognized as a Korean religion. There was no strong and massive anti-Christian campaign afterward. Christianity played its role as a Korean religion.

Beginning of a New Social Culture

Elimination of the Class System

08 Culture

Protestantism entered Korea and greatly contributed to eliminating Korea's class system. This was a symbolic contribution to Korean society and culture. The axes of Korean missions were medial service in hospitals, public education in schools and mission activities of churches. The elimination of the class system in Korea emerged in all these three areas of missions.

The first mission activity in Korea was medical service. Allen was a surgeon and the first to settle down in Korea as a missionary. He was the only medical doctor with Western medical knowledge in Korea at that time. He treated a politician, Min Byungik who was seriously wounded during Gapshinjungbyeon* immediately after his settlement in Korea. This was a good opportunity for him to advertise the effect of Western medicine. Allen eventually established Jejung Hospital, the first modern hospital in Korea and also a medical school in the hospital.

Jejung Hospital was established to treat poor people and transfer Western medicine to Koreans. With these purposes Jejung Hospital provided all Koreans with medical service regardless their class backgrounds. It was of particular significance that the hospital recruited female medical missionaries and opened a women's hospital considering the Korean social environment that did not allow male medical staff to treat female patients. This kind of effort contributed to changing people's understanding of medical service and sanitation. It also contributed to changing people's understanding of the class system. The elimination of the class system began here in the hospital.

Jejung Hospital welcomed and treated anyone, from high class intellectuals and wealthy people to poor people and even people from the lowest class. This practice was the platform for the elimination of the class system. In particular,

---

* This is a political coup organized by a few politicians who wanted to open the country and oust the politicians who were opposing the opening on December 4, 1894.

the hospital trained Korean medical staff and expanded medical service to more people in society. At the same time, it tried to transfer the leadership of the hospital to Koreans and the class system was dramatically overcome in this process.

There was a strict class system dividing Korean society into three at that time; the upper class called Yangban, the middle class of ordinary people called Sangmin and the lowest class called Cheonmin. The class system was especially strict in Seoul as it was the capital city and there were separate settlements where people from same classes lived together. There was a village called Gwanjagol where people from the lowest class were living. These people were butchers and were despised as not humans. A child in the village was attending a church and his father was seriously ill. Samuel F. Moore, a missionary heard about the child and his father, and went to the village with Oliver R. Avision who was Emperor Gojong's doctor. The father who had medical treatment for the first time in his life was deeply touched and recovered not long after.

The father continuously encouraged his son to attend the church and he himself went to the church with courage. Many church members opposed his attendance and refused to attend worship with him. But Moore supported him strongly and the father was encouraged very much by Moore's support. He devoted himself to missions and at the same time, was engaged in the movement to liberate lowest class people.

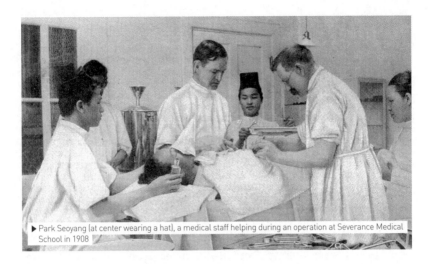
▶ Park Seoyang (at center wearing a hat), a medical staff helping during an operation at Severance Medical School in 1908

This lowest class father's child entered Severance School and became one of the first seven Korean medical doctors. His name was Park Seoyang and he was admired by people for his medical knowledge and skills. His father overcame a lot of difficulties and served his church as an elder. These two stories that a butcher was elected as a church elder and a butcher's son became a medical doctor were like a miracle at that time. This was a good example that Christianity made efforts to bring changes to Korean society and its class system.

Church missions also made a huge contribution to education in Korea. There were a lot of orphans who had lost parents to epidemic and had been born out of wedlock and abandoned when Protestant missionaries first came to Korea. Missionaries therefore established schools that could take care of these orphans. Then they established schools for boys and girls separately. There was no class discrimination in these schools. It was natural that the students who were educated in these schools began working in society and leading social changes.

Above all, the schools and modern education system established by missionaries and churches contributed to providing equal education opportunities to ordinary children who were not from high-class families. They could study in middle schools and continue studying at colleges thanks to this formulated education system. Social changes through this education system emerged in various areas from social structures to individual attitudes. Churches' devotion to education contributed to cultivating human resources who could lead social changes. This again had a great influence on diverse areas of Korean society and spread all over the country.

Churches also made a great contribution to Korean society through their mission activities. At the beginning, mission activities focused on organizing worship services and bible studies, teaching children at Sunday schools and building churches. Churches were very attentive to their neighboring areas and active in taking care of people. Churches played a leading role in building new communities through this kind of activity and also created a new church culture. New religious communities were built around churches and discrimination against lower social classes gradually disappeared.

Churches translated the bible into Korean,

published hymn books and taught church members. In particular, churches established the Christian Literature Society of Korea and published and distributed religious books. This contributed to spreading a culture of reading to all social classes and popularizing Western music. Christian books used principally Korean and this also enormously contributed to developing Korean literature. The spread of Korean literature challenged the high class culture based on Chinese literature and resulted in the gradual disappearance of cultural divides. Christian publications targeted the general public and therefore had to use Korean. This was possible because there was already a structure of Korean characters that was called Hoonminjeongum* and which was shared with and used by the general public.

Churches also engaged in youth activities that were mostly led by YMCA and YWCA. These activities clarified the meaning of youth and spread a cultural movement focusing on and for young people. Churches were especially interested in organizing mission activities for young people and awakening those who could play major roles in changing society. In fact, these young people who were related to churches led Korean society in diverse areas. Churches gradually and constantly led social changes by influencing policies and systems, and at the same time, people's minds.

* This is the old name of Hangul, the Korean writing system. This was invented by King Sejong in 1443 but was not welcomed by intellectuals who insisted on using Chinese characters and in fact, refused to use it. It was mostly used by low class people until the early twentieth century.

YMCA was established not by the suggestion of missionaries but by the request of 150 Korean young people. This was one example of young people's voluntary action that emerged in the process of young people's organized activities. This kind of youth action was very new in Korea at that time and most of the young people who led this action and many other people who worked with these young people participated in breaking up the class system and in introducing social changes. The disappearance of the class system in Korean society through Christian missions was the foundation of building a new culture in Korea.

Early Christian Music

09 Culture

In the 1890s and 1900s Koreans knew almost nothing about Western music. In 1923, the first Korean book about Western music, *Umakdaehae* was published to help church choirs and Christians understand Western music and read musical scores. Koreans were obviously unfamiliar with Western music and had difficulties to follow Western melodies. It was even more difficult to listen to and sing in four-part chorus. Eli M. Mowry was a teacher of Soongsil School in Pyongyang and organized a choir at Pyongyang Jangdaehyun Church which was the first choir in Korea. She mentioned that it was very difficult to have the chorus established in Korea.

"In general, Koreans are not familiar with listening to music with four parts. One person commented after listening to our school's vocal quartet that it could have been better if one had sung and others had been in silence. Another person mentioned that he really wanted to run way from listening to the thirty people singing in the chorus."

In spite of this challenge, Korean church music contributed to educating many musicians and sent them out to society in the early years. Western music was introduced by missionaries and people who were attracted to organ music, hymns and chorus music began to learn Western music. Kim Insik was one of them and was recognized as the pioneer of Western music and church music in Korea afterward.

"At that time, anyone who wanted to learn Western music had to start with church music. It was because Western music was introduced and played by missionaries. I was also attracted to hymns that were played by organs and sung by people. I entered Soongduk School at eleven and eagerly learned Western songs."

Kim Insik composed Hakdoga which is recognized as the first Western song composed in Korea. He began going to the church after his uncle, who had been arrested for participating in Donghakdang, a group led by the indigenous Korean religion, Donghak, was released and saved his life because of Christianity. He was a child and found church music very interesting. He then entered Soongduk School and began to learn Changga, or Western songs. He entered Soongsil Middle School at sixteen and wanted to learn music more systematically. He learned vocal music from William B. Hunt's wife and Velma L. Snook, the headmaster of Soongui Girls' School.

Kim Insik had a great talent and passion for music. He collected money together with four students in his dormitory and bought an organ from a missionary. He practiced organ so hard that students in the dormitory complained a lot. He eventually was kicked out of the dormitory. He could play organ very well in his third grade and the headmaster asked him to teach music classes to students in the first and second grades. His passion for music was not limited to organ. He also learned cornet from Graham Lee and studied violin by himself. He could play hymns after four days of self-teaching and Graham Lee and other missionaries were very much surprised by his talent and passion.

Kim Insik's talent and passion for music were known and appreciated by people when he went to Seoul at the age of twenty two and became a career educator in 1907. He greatly contributed to the development of Korean modern music. He wanted to go abroad for studying but made up his mind to work as the first Korean music teacher to meet the demands of the times. He began teaching at Soongsil Middle School and afterward taught music in many other schools such as Giho, Jinmyung, Osung, Kyungshin and Baejae.

In 1909, the first music school, Joyang Gurakbu, was established and Kim Insik began to teach there. He educated Lee Sangjun and Hong Nanpa who became famous musicians afterward. This music school changed to Chosun Jeongak School. The official purpose of this school was to teach people both Korean and Western music, and to encourage them to be proud of Korean music. But the goal behind it was to comfort people who had lost their country. This school was the first music school that taught both Western and traditional Korean music. Kim Insik taught music and later chorus at the YMCA. He also made a chorus based in Jonggyo Church. This chorus began with a men's chorus and changed to a mixed chorus, Kyungsung Chorus. This was the beginning of the chorus in Korea.

The men's and women's Kyungsung Chorus was a meaningful trial in Korea. It was very new for Koreans to see women singing in front of an audience at that time. The first Korean choir at Jangdeahyun Church was also a men's choir. It was not socially allowed to hear women's voices outside houses and women could not sing loudly even in the house. In this social environment, women except for prostitutes with special professions could sing loudly only in the church. Churches had sitting arrangements separating men and women, and curtains between the two groups. However, churches were the only public place for women to sing together with men. Women who were forced to be quiet at home and in society could express their humanity through singing only at the church.

In 1886, Ewha School was established and music was considered as an important subject together with bible study in girls' schools. Women learned music in a systematic way in schools and could lead church ceremonies as singers in front of an audience, especially on Christmas and other special days. One example was the Christmas Eve ceremony that was organized by Methodist churches and held at Chungdong Methodist Church on Decembber 24, 1898. It was a big event with 600-700 Christians, and students of Ewha School sang English hymns during the offering time.

"There was a big ceremony the night of December 24 in Chungdong First Methodist Church. Christian brothers and sisters gathered and celebrated together the birth of Jesus Christ. The church was decorated with candles at the top of the bell tower and the ceremony was formal with well-organized rituals…students from Ewha School sang English hymns and offerings were made. There were 600-700 men and women, and all celebrated the birth of Jesus Christ together with great joy."

Women could sing in front of the audience in public gatherings. In the early years of Korean churches music was an important means for women to get out of their forced silence.

Contribution to Maintaining Korean Spirit, Lifestyle and Culture

Christianity's Influence
on Korean Modern Architecture

Christianity had a big influence on Korean society and culture in the process of its development. The legacy continues in many areas of society and culture in Korea. Architecture is not an exception. In the period of its introduction and gradual growth Christianity had a big influence on traditional Korean architecture in many ways across the country.

The physical environment of Korea changed in many ways due to rapidly changing political and social situations. This change was also projected into architecture that often showed in harmony with nature. The modernization of Korean architecture was tried in constructing Suwon Fortress based on pragmatism and importing new ideas from the outside world in the late eighteenth century. New foreign styles of architecture were introduced with Japanese style public buildings, finance buildings, Catholic churches, hotels and factories built by foreign merchants, and churches, schools, hospitals and residences built by Protestant churches in the late nineteenth century and the early twentieth century.

The buildings constructed by Protestant churches were peculiar in terms of importing authentic Western styles of architecture. Christian buildings were different from other buildings constructed in same period because missionaries and Korean Christians would work together throughout the construction. For example, Japan would prefer imperial styles that modified Western styles. The Seoul Train Station and the Hanguk Bank are good examples. By contrast, architectural styles of Christian buildings were chosen by ordinary Koreans and therefore designed in many different ways such as Korean–Western, Western and modern styles of architecture. Gangwha Anglican Church and Onsoori Anglican Church in Gangwha, and Cheongju Anglican Church followed the Korean–Western style and all of them still exist. Chungdong First Methodist Church, Sungdong Church, Daegu Jeil Church, Cheongju Jeil Church and Andong Church chose Gothic style of architecture. However, they clearly opposed the imperial style that was favored by Japan.

Churches represented Christian architecture.

Churches were built in Seoul and other cities that were centers of local missions. Saemoonan Church, Chungdong First Methodist Church, Sungdong Church, Yeongdong Church and Andong Church were built in Seoul. Daegueup Church was built in Daegu, Choryang Church in Busan, Guam Church in Gunsan, Seomoon Church in Jeonju, Yangdong Church in Gwangju, Chungjueup Church in Chungju, Andong Church in Andong, Yanglim Church in Gwangju, Joongang Church in Sooncheon. Solnae Church, Pyongyang Jangdaehyun Church, Seonchuneup Church, Ganggyeeup Church, Sunchunnam Church, Jaeryungeup Church, Pyongyang Changdong Church, Wonsan Church were built in what is now North Korea. These churches built across the country were a cultural stimulus to local societies and at the same time, brought some hope to local people to overcome the Japanese colonialism. In the process of building churches Christians could work together and build close relationships among themselves. They participated in building churches under the leadership of missionaries and Korean pastors, and experienced mutual communication between their Korean spirit and skills and Western ideas. The process of building churches itself was a meaningful, historic event.

Christian schools represented another style of Christian architecture. These schools played an important role in combining Christian spirit and Western education in Korea. At the same time, they had a great influence on Korean modern architecture in terms of their scales, styles and technologies used. Christian schools were built across the country with the systematization of education from elementary to middle and high schools. Baejae School, Ewha School, Kyungshin School, Chungshin School, Baewha School, Yonhee College and Severance Medical School were built in Seoul. Gyesung School and Shingmyung School were built in Daegu, Shingheung School and Gijeon School in Jeonju, Chungmyung Girls' School in Mokpo, Soongil School, Speer Girls' School in Gwangju, Chungnam School in Chungju, Gyemyung School in Andong and Maesan School in Sooncheon. In North Korea area now, Soongsil School in Pyongyang, Boseong Girls' School and Shinsung School in Seonchun, Myungshin School in Jaeryung and Youngsil School in Ganggye were built by Christians. Educational institutions were diversified to include bible schools and kindergartens after the announcement of the Chosun Education Law by the Japanese government. Christian schools played a very important role in educating young people who could contribute to the future of Korean society.

Christian schools mostly chose Korean-Western styles of architecture and at the same time, tried to be friendly to Koreans. Adams Hall and McPherson Hall of Gyesung School in Daegu are good examples that still exist. After the second and third Chosun Education Laws many schools chose Gothic and Georgian styles to have bigger buildings and accommodate more students. Handerson Hall of Gyesung School in Daegu and Underwood Hall, Steamson Hall and Appenzeller Hall of Yonsei University were built with Gothic style. Severance Hall of Chungshin Girls' School in Seoul, Maesan Hall of Maesan

Middle School in Sooncheon, Winsborough Hall of Speer Girls' High School and Purdy Memorial Bible School in Chungju were built with Georgian style. These buildings still exist.

Christian schools influenced many other schools. Joongang School and Korea University were established with independent Korean funds and were built with Gothic style. Christian schools were built for missions and were very different from public schools established by Japan in terms of architectural styles and underlying philosophies. These Christian schools also had a great influence on many private schools that were established by Koreans.

Christian hospitals were established for missions through medical treatments and their main purpose was to provide medical service to Koreans. And yet the fundamental goal was to reach out to Koreans and build close relationships with Koreans before missions.

Regarding architectural styles, Christian hospitals chose Korean–Western style as did Christian schools so that Koreans could feel familiar and friendly with Western hospitals. One example of this style was Duncan Memorial Hospital in Chungju. After the Chosun Medical Law Christian hospitals were built in local cities with Western styles so that they could accommodate basic facilities. These hospitals gradually grew and became major medical institutions.

Christian hospitals were established in many cities. These hospitals were Severance Hospital in Seoul, Dongsan Hospital in Daegu, Jesus Hospital in Jeonju, French Memorial Hospital in Mokpo, Graham Memorial Hospital in Gwangju, Duncan Memorial Hospital in Chungju, Sungso Hospital in Andong and Alexander Hospital in Sooncheon. In present North Korean area Midong Hospital was built in Seonchun and Yonhap Christian Hospital was built in Pyongyang. The construction of hospitals was complicated and demanded detailed designs. These factors greatly contributed to the development of architecture in local cities. Hospitals also made a big contribution to laying a foundation for missions through medical treatments and trips made by hospital staff.

Residences of missionaries were another example that showed the development of architecture. In the early years, missionaries would buy traditional Korean houses and renovate them for their convenient use. Some missionaries built Western style houses and maintained their lifestyles. In local cities, missionaries would buy traditional houses and renovate them, and later build Korean—Western style houses. The examples of these houses are Forsyth Memorial House in Chungju, Switzer House in Daegu and Miller House in Chungju. These houses still remain. In the 1930s, new styles of architecture in the world were introduced to Korea. But the new styles were only chosen by Japanese architects. Only a few Koreans were interested in the new styles. Missionaries preferred Gothic, Georgian and American Colonial styles which formed a separate trend in Korea. Wilson House in Gwangju and Missionary House in Yeonjidong, Seoul show this trend.

This trend can be also seen in many residences of missionaries such as Underwood House in Seoul and Switzer House and Blair House in Daegu. But Moffet House in Pyongyang was built with traditional Korean style and used for a long time without renovation. It is very important to see how architecture can accommodate lifestyles in terms of culture. Missionaries from the Western world had a great influence on Korean Christians and at the same time, on houses and lifestyles. Christian buildings had a big influence on modern architecture in Korea. They contributed to maintaining Korean spirit, culture and lifestyle, and in particular, national identity under the harsh colonial regime of Japan.

Religion

The First Korean Hymnals, Chanmiga & Chanyangga

Christianity was already introduced to Korea through China and Japan before Horace G. Underwood and Henry G. Appenzeller came to Korea. Koreans were already using a Korean bible and translated hymns. Christians who had been baptized in China and Japan were engaged in mission activities and the bible and hymns were spreading in different ways. Seo Sangryun who had established Sorae Church and Baek Hongjun who had started Uiju Church used Chinese hymns following Chinese pronunciations or changing them into Korean pronunciations. At that time, Chinese hymns were simply changed to Korean pronunciations or translated into Korean.

This way of using Chinese hymns was problematic because the hymns were full of Chinese expressions that even Korean intellectuals could not understand, and therefore the meanings of hymns could not be correctly shared with people.

English hymns were translated into Korean and used after the official arrival of missionaries. There were more than fifty English hymns translated into Korean before the first Korean hymns such as *Chanmiga* in the Methodist church(1892) and *Changyangga* in the Presbyterian church(1894) were published. But there is no detailed information about which English songs were used. These English hymns were translated and used one by one, and Koreans therefore did not have much opportunity to learn the hymns. Missionaries could not visit all the churches across the country every Sunday and Christians could learn translated hymns only at bible studies that would take place once or twice a year. Melodies of English hymns were not correctly followed because Koreans were not familiar with Western music and could not have enough time to learn hymns perfectly. William C. Kerr mentioned that "I have never heard Koreans who could correctly sing hymns other than well trained musicians."

More people needed hymn books as mission activities were getting more active and Christians were increasing in number. The Methodist church took the first step and collected twenty seven hymns and published the first Korean hymnbook *Chanmiga* in May 1888. This hymnbook was edited by

George H. Jones, who had been working at Baejae School and had been devoted to bible teaching and mission work in Incheon since his arrival in Korea. It was only published for use in Methodist churches and musical scores were not included. The main purpose of the hymnbook was to have major subjects of the bible arranged in a comprehensive way and to prepare hymns that could be used for traditional Christian events. This hymnbook was revised several times afterward and missionaries shared their concerns about translated hymns in the preface of the 1895 version.

"Can appropriate and understandable hymns be made through translation? We do not think so. We reached this conclusion after spending several days to translate one hymn properly and experiencing imperfection with one translated line. There must be Korean composers and lyricists soon who can sing and write down their own songs coming from the bottom of their hearts and share them with Korean Christians."

Additionally, the Presbyterian Church and the Methodist Church agreed to publish a hymnbook together and Jones and Underwood took responsibility for the task. But Jones stayed away too long on a visit home to the US. Underwood could not wait any longer for Jones's return and published a hymnbook, *Chanyangga* unilaterally. The Methodist Church criticized Underwood's unilateral decision and rejected the use of this hymnbook. It decided to revise *Chanmiga* and to use it. There was another problem: Underwood had included the words, 'Jehovah' and 'Father' in the hymnbook though these words had not been agreed on with the Methodist Church. Underwood however did not include the word, 'God' that the Methodist Church had insisted to use. The Methodist Church could not accept *Chanyangga* because of this disagreement.

In spite of this conflict, *Chanyangga* is recognized as an important book in Korean Western music history because it had four-part musical scores for the first time in Korea. It is also understood as the first well-published hymnbook in terms of its size(117 hymns) and form. But all the musical scores that were found in the first edition of *Chanyangga* disappeared from the second edition. There were only lyric lines in Korean because most Koreans hardly understood musical scores and hymnbooks with musical scores were not usually used. In fact, the first Korean book on theory and practice of Western music, *Umakdaehae* was published for choirs and Christians who could not read musical scores in 1923. Thus it was hard to find Koreans who could understand Western musical scores in the 1890s. Underwood was eager to introduce Western musical structures and theories to Korea as soon as possible. But Koreans were not ready yet to accommodate his passion.

On the other hand, all the hymns except for seven were translations from other languages into Korean in *Chanyangga*. Underwood shared his difficulty to translate English into Korean saying "the number of characters does not fit in melodies⋯." Gale also sighed looking at hymns and lyrics in *Chanmiga* and *Chanyangga*. He said "it is very unnatural because Korean lyric lines are uncomfortably written to fit in Western melodies and lyrics. There is lack of wholeness due to the absence of spiritual inspiration. Hymns therefore do not have original meanings." It was a big problem that melodies and lyrics did not fit with each other. Frederich S. Miller participated in the translation and editing of the hymns and had difficulties with certain tunes. He mentioned as follows.

> *"The biggest challenge was that Korean did not go with weakness and strength rhythms. There is no Korean word that has an accent on the second syllable. Then I had to put all one-syllable words at the beginning of every line. This caused simple lyrical lines. It could have been better if I had pulled out all hymns with weakness and strength rhythms."*

English has articles and English hymns use incomplete bars to give accents to nouns in the second syllables. But there are no incomplete bars in traditional Korean music because Korean does not have definite and indefinite articles. Therefore translators of English hymns put one-syllable Korean words in article parts of incomplete bars. The natural result was that some hymns were not well-adapted for singing and understanding meaning.

In spite of translation problems that missionaries struggled with for a long time, hymns played a very important role to enhance Koreans' literacy. All lyrical lines of hymns were in Korean that was much simpler than biblical sentences. They were also easier to memorize. For this reason, hymns were more useful to help Koreans learn Hangul(the Korean alphabet) than the bible was. Koreans who understood neither Western musical scores nor Hangul first learned hymns by memorizing lyrics. They then could easily learn Hangul by looking at lyrical lines in hymns and matching them with memorized ones.

"Church members easily learned hymns by memorizing lyrics. It was much easier for them than learning the bible. Hymnbooks soon became the most popular reader. It was interesting that some writers chose passages in the bible and composed musical poems."

It was obvious that hymnbooks were becoming one of the most important textbooks for learning Hangul. On that matter, there was an interesting episode relating to hymnbook publishing. In 1935, the Presbyterian Church published *New Hymnbook* but did not follow the unified standard of Hangul decided by Korean Linguistic Association. Some people pointed out that it was a cultural problem.

"…it is because Christian publications play an important role together with school textbooks in the process of cultural development…the recently published New Hymnbook is considered one of the first big publications by churches…

however the New Hymnbook strangely has many problems and does not follow new spelling rules⋯the Christian culture that has played the leading role in the process of modernizing Korean culture is anti-national these days."

As a result of social criticism, the Presbyterian Church decided to apply the unified standard to the *New Hymnbook* in 1937. *Donga Daily* welcomed this decision and on September 19, 1937 it published as follows.

"The bible and hymnbook have greatly contributed to the development of Christian culture and also to the eradication of illiteracy and to cultural development in the era of Korea's modernization. The churches' decision to follow the unified standard of Hangul will contribute to recruiting more than 300,000 people who can participate in supporting and spreading the unified standard of Hangul."

Lost Dream of One National Church

Discussion of Korea Christ Church in 1905

12 Religion

Protestantism was introduced to Korea late compared to its introduction in other countries. Mission organizations in Korea therefore wanted to apply the methods and experiences they had in other countries to Korea. But their experiences in China, India and Japan could not reflect the Korean situation. This reality was especially challenging when they began discussing the Korea Christ Church in 1905. The Korea Christ Church meant an indigenous, independent church in Korea that would be free from any external and denominational influence. The idea was as follows.

"The missionaries from Presbyterian and Methodist churches organized a committee in Seoul on June 25, 1905 and unanimously agreed to William D. Reynolds's motion. The motion said "…now it is the time to build one national church and name it Korea Christ Church." The General Council of Evangelical Missions could not refuse this motion and decided to make efforts to build a united evangelical church in Korea."

The foundation of one national church was first suggested by William Reynolds. But discussion of the united Korean church was rather natural considering the ultimate goal of missions that the missionaries understood. The common goal of world missions at that time was to establish "a self-supporting, self-propagating and self-governing native church." It meant that the ultimate goal of world missions was to encourage indigenous churches to have the ownership of all operations as soon as possible, to be not objects of missions but subjects of missions, and to build indigenous, independent churches so that they could deal with all church matters by themselves.

Many missionaries who worked in Korea in the early years shared this ultimate goal of missions. They realized that different denominations did not have any meaning in Korea. They did not emphasize denominations in Korea and tried to develop collaborative mission programs considering the Korean situation. But the Council of Presbyterian Mission in Korea wanted to build its own church in Korea.

This was far from the ultimate goal of missions, the foundation of one indigenous church, shared by world churches. But there were also Presbyterian missionaries who supported the idea of building not a Presbyterian denomination but a united Korean church together with other denominations. At this time, the US Northern Presbyterian Church had a meeting celebrating the 20th anniversary of Korea missions. In this meeting one missionary expressed his idea as follows.

"I have a dream of building one organized church that could lead Christian families, Christian societies, Christian leaders and Christian territories, and manage and influence all of these. I think that church could be one united church of Christ that does not belong to any denomination but is operated by well trained and selected local pastors."

This idea was discussed in detail and different ideas about the foundation of the Korea Christ Church were shared in 1905. 150 missionaries agreed to build one united church in Korea. This showed their vision and passion for one church. The discussion about one church was shared with many people in Korea and others from mission fields around the world affirmed its possibility.

The next thing that had to be considered was the name of the united church. The name that missionaries had decided after discussions was the Korea Christ Church. This was the officially decided name by the General Council of Protestant Evangelical Missions in Korea that had been established to build a united church in Korea. This organization had the goal of founding a united evangelical church in Korea. The term 'evangelical' here meant 'Protestant', and was a general term used for Protestant churches at that time.

But the dream of building one united church in Korea was not accomplished. A few reasons could be considered: Presbyterian churches could not make the final decision before the establishment of an independent presbytery in Korea; Presbyterian and Methodist churches had different histories; and it was not a realistic idea considering their separate missions based on different denominational backgrounds. But the most important reason was the differing positions of mission departments and missionaries on the foundation of "a self-supporting, self-propagating and self-governing native church."

They shared the basic ideas but had different understandings of the goals. The mission departments were concerned about the similar trials and results that had taken place in other countries. In the cases of indigenous churches in Asia, in China, India and Japan, and in other regions the identity of Christianity was often challenged, according to their understanding. This kind of concern was expressed as follows.

"There is a strong tendency for the missionaries who were trained in specific denominations to feel

they must follow their denominations' ideas in foreign mission fields. On the other hand, each Christian community has a right to make decisions for its own interest and this right must be protected. But it is not easy to ignore that there can be some risks. These can be serious sometimes. We cannot say that churches in Japan, China and India were evangelically built. God could do so. But who could easily determine the healthiness of churches?"

In 1905, the General Council of Protestant Evangelical Missions in Korea was founded to realize the idea of building one united church. Detailed discussions on this idea began in the General Conference of the US Northern Methodist Church. Methodist missionaries invited other denominations' missionaries and provided them with an opportunity to talk about the issues of joint missions in detail. At that time, Korean churches were rapidly growing but missionaries had difficulty keeping pace with Korean churches because of lack of financial and human resources.

In the General Conference William M. Baird made a speech and emphasized the importance of joint efforts for education programs in Korea. He presented the example of Kyungshin School and Baejae School, which had united and become one of the best education institutions in Korea. He also explained a new hospital plan of Mary M. Cutler who was then in charge of the Methodist Women's Hospital. He emphasized that the plan could achieve the best results with the collaboration of the Presbyterian Church. Mary R. Hillman who was in charge of Ewha School also argued the need for collaboration with the Presbyterian Church to expand facilities and have an efficient operation. Other missionaries actively agreed to these suggestions. The General Conference selected members to discuss and carry out collaborative work, and started discussions with the Presbyterian Church.

The preparation was carried out quickly. On June 26, immediately after the General Conference, Presbyterian and Methodist missionaries gathered at Dalziel A. Bunker's house to discuss future collaboration and decide their goals of collaboration. They decided two important things. One was to found one united Protestant church in Korea and call it 'Korea Christ Church.' The other was that all Christian entities in Korea must work together for mission programs in Korea. They shared a vision and a passion for one united church in Korea and presented many positive ideas including the establishment of a council of Protestant mission, a suggestion from William B. Scranton.

Missionaries organized a joint committee of Presbyterian and Methodist churches to carry on collaborative work and decided to hold a gathering inviting all Protestant missionaries. This gathering took place in the chapel of Ewha School on September 11. Underwood was elected as the chair and Bunker as the general manager in this gathering. In the following presentations and discussions Scranton suggested organizing the Evangelical Council of Missions. This motion was agreed upon by participants and the organization was established in this gathering, with the participants as the first members. Underwood and Bunker decided to maintain their positions, and a committee was organized to make the rules and regulations of the new organization.

Missionaries discussed structural issues and doctrines in preparation to build one united Protestant church belonging to the Evangelical Council of Missions. They gradually faced big and small difficulties. In 1910, they reached the conclusion that they could pursue realistic harmony as they established churches in Korean society rather than pursuing a perfect structural unity and one united church. They also concluded that it could be more desirable to focus on eliminating potential problems that could be obstacles to the united church and on generating tangible results. At this stage, the idea to found one united church was almost given up and the organization's name changed to the Federal Council of Protestant Missions in 1911.

The collaboration and unity of Presbyterian and Methodist churches failed but the Federal Council of Protestant Missions contributed to promoting collaborative work in mission programs and also played a leading role in the ecumenical movement in Korea. Detailed contributions are found in the following.

"In Seoul, Baejae School of the Methodist Church and Kyungshin School of the Presbyterian Church tried joint operation. Severance Hospital and Severance Medical School became united institutions and Pierson Memorial Bible School was established without denominational background. In Pyongyang, the Presbyterian Church and Methodist Church together ran Soongsil School and Soongui Girls' School, and Gihol Hospital of the Methodist Church became a united institution. Chanmiga of the Methodist Church and Chanyangga of the Presbyterian Church were united and newly published as Hymn Book. The Christ Newspaper of the Presbyterian Church and the Christian Paper of the Methodist Church were united. English magazines, the Korea Methodist and the Korea Field of the Presbyterian Church were united and became the Korean Mission Field."

In particular, collaboration in education programs was prominent. Collaboration was especially important for higher education. Yonhee College could not be established with only the support of the US Northern Presbyterian Church. The US Northern and Southern Methodist Churches also supported the college so it could open. The college would later become a high quality education institute with the support of the US Southern Presbyterian Church and the Presbyterian Church of Canada.

The Pierson Memorial Bible School was founded for the theological education of lay people without denominational background and educated many church leaders. The Federal Council of Protestant Missions had meetings in this school. This organization made a big contribution to many united programs including medical service. But only missionaries could have membership in the organization.

Missionaries and Korean church leaders had different positions regarding the Japanese colonial rule. First of all, they had different ideas about the political situation and related issues. On this topic, missionaries gradually faced the issues they could not deal with. The Korean church leaders had to respond to changes in society and among churches. The leaders of the Presbyterian Church and the Methodist Church eventually organized the Korean Church Federal Council in 1918. This was the first united organization founded not by missionaries but by Korean churches. This meant that the Korean churches took the lead of the ecumenical movement.

The Federal Council of Protestant Missions and the Korean Church Federal Council co-existed, but there was a growing need for one united ecumenical body. As a result, a discussion on the unity of the two organizations began in 1922. On September 24, 1924, the Korean National Christian Council was founded in Saemoonan Church.

Sorae Church,
Saemoonan Church,
and Chungdong First Methodist Church

Sorae Church

Protestantism was officially introduced to Korea upon the arrival of Horace N. Allen, a missionary and medical doctor from the US in 1884. Sorae Church, established in Songchun-ri, Daegu-myeon, Jangyeon-gun, Hwanghae-do, was the first Protestant church in Korea. Sorae, the village where this Presbyterian church was located had been named 'Solsaem' which means a fountain beside a pine tree. This name Solsaem changed to Solnae, which means a spring beside a pine tree, and then to Sorae.

There were about seventy households when Christianity was introduced to the village. In traditional Korean villages, people used to live with others from the same family lines. But Sorae was a unique village where people from different family lines were living together. Yet one particular family, the Seo family, moved into Sorae in the 1870s and introduced Christianity to the village.

Seo Sangryun with his brother Seo Kyungjo went to Manchuria, China for trading in 1878 and caught a fever. He was treated by John MacIntyre, a Scottish missionary who was visiting Manchuria. He then met John Ross and was baptized. He participated in missionaries' translation work of the bible together with Lee Ungchan, Baek Hongjun, and Kim Ginki. They were all baptized later with Seo Sangryun. This translated Korean bible was published in 1883. He and his colleagues returned to Korea with some copies of this bible and started mission activities. They were detected at a border checkpoint on their way back to Korea, but fortunately they escaped from the scene and saved ten copies of the bible.

They escaped to Sorae. In 1884 and 1885, families of Seo Sangryun and Seo Kyungjo also moved to Sorae. These two families began gathering and worshipping together beginning in 1884. This was the first Christian congregation in Korea. In September 1885 Underwood visited Sorae and baptized these Christians.

Sorae congregation gathered in a house. It was a traditional Korean house without any structural changes. Church members only put a cross on the rooftop to show that the house was a church. Sorae was a remarkable, symbolic birthplace of Christianity in Korea. In the early years, it was important for missionaries to visit Sorae. Underwood from the US Northern Presbyterian Church, Malcolm C. Fenwick, a Canadian who established East Asia Christian Church(now Baptist church) and William J. McKenzie, a Canadian missionary, established churches and lived in Sorae. McKenzie did not leave Sorae and was martyred there. After his death many missionaries would visit Sorae and Mckenzie's house when they visited Korea.

Sorae Church was the Christian center for the region. Dozens of churches in Songwha, Eunyul, Poongcheon, Moonwha, Haeju and Ongjin were established following the model of Sorae Church. In 1902, churches and their members in Sorae and neighboring areas suffered from a series of attacks by Catholics. Catholicism entered Korea about one hundred years earlier than Protestantism. Some Catholics were jealous of the rapid increase of Protestant churches. They manipulated the power of French priests and attacked Christians and tried to loot churches in Hwanghae-do. Underwood was informed of these incidents and the churches' suffering, and he requested the Korean government to intervene in the situation. The suffering of Christians and churches in Hwanghae-do ended thanks to Underwood's help and the government's intervention. In 1907, after graduating from Pyongyang Theological Seminary, Seo

Sangryun became the first pastor in Sorae Church. He then went to Seoul and worked with Underwood in Saemoonan Church. In Sorae Church Kim Duheon, Jang Unggon and Huh Gan worked as pastors. Sorae Church was called a cradle of Christianity in Korea.

Saemoonan Church

Saemoonan Church is now a member of the Presbyterian Church of Korea. This church is very close to Chung-dong area in Jongno-gu where Chungdong Mission Department was located. It was the first structured Protestant church in Korea. On September 27, 1897, Underwood started the church with Seo Sangryun and Baek Hongjoon. This day was not Sunday but Tuesday. Fourteen joined the first gathering. Thirteen out of them were in contact with Seo Sangryun who was engaged in mission activities and bible sales and introduced Christianity to them. Therefore, they were already Christians.

The beginning of Saemoonan Church was the result of many people's efforts, in particular: missionaries of the British Bible Society who were based in Manchuria, China; Korean Christians who were engaged in mission activities and bible sales; and Underwood, a missionary of the US Northern Presbyterian Church. Saemoonan Church was originally called Chungdong Presbyterian Church or Seodaemoon Presbyterian Church. Then it was finally called Saemoonan Church because the church was near to Saemoon.*

Saemoonan Church began in a room of a house that Underwood had bought for his own use. It was more like a home church that gathered in a private house. In this home church Underwood's Korean teacher No Dosa was baptized in July 1886. In the early years, the church could not grow because Underwood was in charge of so many things. In 1886, Guse School, which had begun with bringing and teaching orphans, expanded and changed to Kyungshin School. This school became the foundation of education business and eventually contributed to establishing Yonsei Universty. The development of these schools also contributed to the growth of Saemoonan Church.

Bible studies, one of the unique characteristics of Korean churches, began in Saemoonan Church. A bible study began in 1890 following the strong tradition of Presbyterian churches that focused on the bible. People gathered and read the bible together. In 1892, Saemoonan Church hosted a bible study meeting with the participation of Christians from all over the country. Sixteen participated in the meeting and all the participants had a good knowledge of the bible and were ready to answer any questions about the bible.

The construction of Saemoonan Church began

* Saemoon is also called Donuimoon or Seodaemoon. This was one of four big gates in Seoul. It was rebuilt in 1711 and people called it saemoon which means 'new gate.' It was destroyed by Japan in 1915 to construct a road.

in 1895. Daniel L. Gifford and Hong Jeonghu were in charge of the entire work. The church was built in a traditional Korean house style and with the devotion and labor of church members. At that time, the wages of ordinary Koreans were about four dollars a month and church members offered 250 dollars in total for the construction. After the construction, Saemoonan Church opened eighteen bible study classrooms in Seoul and actively engaged in mission activities. New churches such as Seokyodong Church and Kimpo Church in the west of Seoul, and Youngdeungpo Church and Siheung Church in the south of Seoul were established with the active mission work of Saemoonan Church. In 1907, the number of members in Saemoonan Church was 600. Due to its rapid growth, Saemoonan Church could not accommodate all the members and began constructing a new church building nearby Kyunghee Palace in 1907. On May 22, 1910, the new church building was completed, accommodating Calvinistic theology with simple architectural design and interior decoration.

In 1910, Seo Kyungjo assumed the position of mission pastor at Underwood's invitation and in 1911, he became a co-worker of Underwood who was the head pastor. In 1911, Cha Jaemyung was invited to a church in Pyongbuk because of Saemoonan Church's close relationship with the region. Cha Jaemyung then started working as the first Korean pastor in charge in Saemoonan Church in 1920. Church activities were getting more energetic with the assumption of leadership by Korean pastors in all departments such as Sunday school, women's gatherings, kindergarten, and the choir. Saemoonan Church was a church rooted in the northwestern region of the Korean peninsula and once was involved in a scandal when pastors from Seoul and the northwestern region confronted each other in the 1930s.

After Korea's independence from the Japanese colonial rule, Saemoonan Church played an important role as one of the mother churches in Korea. The church hosted many meetings and continuously grew even during the Korean War. It grew especially remarkable during Rev. Kang, Shinmyung's leadership from 1955 to 1981. Saemoonan Church played its own role as one of the early churches in Korea.

Chungdong First Methodist Church

This church was the first structured church of the Korean Methodist Church. The church was begun on October 9, 1887 by Henry G. Appenzeller, the first missionary of the US Northern Methodist Church to Korea. The church began in Chung-dong where the church is still located. Appenzeller established Baejae School, a Christian modern school in response to the Koreans' wishes in 1885. He then established Chungdong Church two years after the school. In the early years, Methodists constructed churches following Western style architecture in contrast to Presbyterian churches that had traditional Korean housing styles. Chungdong First Methodist Church was the first

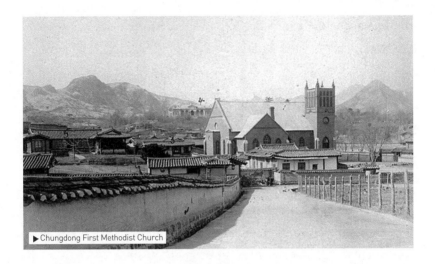

▶Chungdong First Methodist Church

Methodist church having Western style architecture. Especially in the early years the church could grow because Baejae School and Ewha School were nearby.

Chungdong First Methodist Church engaged in diverse mission activities responding to the request to modernize Korea. It actively participated in the modernization movement and the anti-Japan national independence movement along with its mission activities. It therefore was recognized as one of the centers of these two movements. Seo Jaepil returned to Korea from exile and established Dokniphyuphoe which means 'association of independence' in 1896. It was the first organization focusing on Korea's independence. He stayed in Appenzeller's house and had a close relationship with Chungdong First Methodist Church and Baejae School. In 1896, he started printing out Doknipsinmun which means 'independence newspaper' and worked on Sammunsa(The Trilingual Press) in the basement of Baejae School. He also started studying world geography, history and politics in Baejae School in the same year.

In 1896, Hyupsunghoe was organized in Baejae School which included discussions and education programs and No Byungseon, Lee Seungman, and Shin Heungwoo – all young members of Chungdong First Methodist Church – played leading roles in the organization. The youth group of the church was exposed to external threats and pressure because many progressive people were members. It was dissolved as a result of its campaign against the Ulsa Agreement* in 1905.

The construction of the church began in 1895 and finished in 1897. It had a simple reinterpretation of Gothic style of architecture and the altar was facing due west. It was dedicated on December 26, 1897 and became an important Seoul attraction together with Myungdong Cathedral.

The church was also the center of the women's movement in the early years because many students of Ewha School and people related to Ewha School were involved. These people participated in diverse social movements such as campaigns against possession of concubines, early marriages and trading of girls, and the campaign for the promotion of women's education through the church's youth group.

---

* It is a Japan–Korea agreement that Japan forced Korea to sign that aimed to deprive Korea of Korean diplomatic rights.

The choir of the church was famous for its high quality music because most members of the choir were students of Baejae School and Ewha School, and students of Yonhee College and Ewha Women's College volunteered as choir directors. In the 1920s Mary E. Young, the Director of the Music Department of Ewha Women's College, directed the choir. This period was recognized as the golden age of the choir.

Lee Pilju, the pastor in charge at Chungdong First Methodist Church was one of thirty three leaders of the March First Movement in 1919. Park Dongwan, an elder of the church, was also one of them. Kim Jinho, one of the associate pastors in the church and Jeong Dukseong, an elder, also made a great contribution to the movement. Hong Ho, a member of the church's youth group, made leaflets and shared the news and information about the independence movement with people. As a result, many church members were sent to prison and the church had to be suspended until the autumn of 1919 under the close surveillance of the Japanese Government-General.

In 1945, the Methodist church was divided into two groups because of a conflict between pro-reconstruction and pro-growth churches. But Chungdong First Methodist Church maintained its role as one of the mother churches and led Methodist churches to a reunion, hosting in the church a joint general assembly in 1949. During the Korean War the church was seriously damaged by bombing. In 1976, the first church building was designated as a historical spot by the Korean government.

The church constructed a new church building and finished the work on April 15, 1979. The church is still involved in diverse mission activities with prisons, business groups and churches around the world.

Beyond Denomination, Toward Missions

Collaboration of Missionaries

▨▨▨▨▨▨▨▨▨▨▨▨▨▨

14 Religion

Different denominations in Korea were introduced by American missionaries. Korean churches were under a heavy influence of denominationalism from the beginning. Missionaries from different denominations planted their own denominations in Korea. This means that Korean churches began not as one big church but as divided churches. Korean churches therefore needed an ecumenical movement from the beginning.

Most of the Western missionaries came from the US. There were more than 1,500 missionaries in Korea during the sixty years from the fall of 1884 when Horace N. Allen arrived in Korea to summer of 1945 when all the missionaries were deported. 70 percent of them were American missionaries. In particular, among these American missionaries 45.5 percent were from the Presbyterian Church and 28.3 percent were from the Methodist Church. These two churches had a huge human resource pool comparing to other denominations. This means that the map of Korean churches was drawn by Presbyterian and Methodist churches from the beginning. This also means that these two churches led collaborative activities in the early years. Other denominations which started missions in Korea later could not take the lead in mission activities and were rather excluded from collaborative work.

Missionaries worked together in Korea. This was an inevitable choice for them facing the unfamiliar environment in Korea. Korea was like a wilderness to be cultivated and missionaries could not find enough human resources. They had to collaborate. In addition, they could not find many Westerners in Korea and naturally got to know each other and be friends. They were also greatly influenced by the internationalism and inter-denominationalism that were developed by the Protestant churches' mission movement.

One of the most prominent collaborative activities of missionaries was their effort to establish one Korean church regardless of denominational backgrounds. In 1905, four mission departments of the US Northern Presbyterian Church,

US Southern Presbyterian Church, Presbyterian Church in Canada and Presbyterian Church of Australia, and two mission departments of the US Northern Methodist Church and US Southern Methodist Church together established the General Council of Protestant Evangelical Missions in Korea. This organization stood together for one church in Korea in the future. This church would be "one native evangelical church." They even discussed the name of this church, Korea Christ Church or Church of Christ. There would have been one unified church in Korea if their idea had been realized. But their idea could not be realized because the mission departments of their churches back home that had sent them to Korea for mission could not find any reason to establish one unified church in Korea. On the other hand, not every missionary agreed to this idea. On the Korean side, there was nobody who could play a leadership role and the establishment of one church remained a dream in the history of the Korean church.

The General Council of Protestant Evangelical Missions in Korea that led diverse collaborative activities was the beginning of the ecumenical movement in Korea. The translation of the bible, the publishing business of Chosun Christian Publishing and the integration of periodicals were conducted under the management of the council. They also published *Korea Mission Field*(1905), *Christian Newspaper*(1906) and the common hymnbook(1908).

Another prominent collaborative activity of

missionaries in the early years was the community arrangement for missions led by the mission departments of Presbyterian and Methodist churches. Community arrangement was first agreed between the US Northern Methodist Church and the US Northern Presbyterian Church in 1892. According to the agreement, the mission departments of the two churches shared the ports and cities where the population was more than 5,000. In case of a population of less than 5,000, the mission department that had already established a branch could exclusively have the area for missions. They also agreed on eight clauses including the request for a person who wanted to change his/her denomination to bring a recommendation from the former church. This agreement was not accepted at the mission department meeting of the US Northern Methodist Church held in August 1893. But the clauses in the agreement and community arrangement were recognized as principles by the mission departments of the two churches and other churches. The competition and overlapping investment of the mission departments gradually disappeared thanks to the agreement. But other churches were excluded from the agreement. It was possible that other churches could call it a big two-mission agreement.

The third prominent move was the establishment of the Korea National Christian Council which is the root of the National Council of Churches in Korea(NCCK). This was a church council that the Presbyterian Church of Korea, Korea Methodist Church, four mission departments of Presbyterian churches, two mission departments of Methodist churches, British Bible Society and YMCA Korea participated in. This council agreed on principles to respect denominational identities and doctrines. These principles were developed to recognize different theological backgrounds and at the same time to seek Christians' solidarity and collaboration.

The collaboration of missionaries in the early years is a precious historical legacy in Korea where denominational characteristics are strong. This legacy that contributed to mission work and collaborative activities must be maintained and passed on to next generations. Denominationalism and individualism in Korean churches must be eradicated for the healthy environment of the entire Korean church. But one important thing must be pointed out: that the missionaries' collaborative activities much like today's ecumenical movement were limited to Presbyterian and Methodist churches, and these collaborations were sometimes obstacles to other churches that entered Korea later. It was desirable that Presbyterian and Methodist churches tried to make one church. But it would not have been positive for the growth of churches if this had been realized. There were cases in Western churches that the integration of denominations and churches did not contribute to the growth of the churches but caused the decline of the churches for some reason.

Opening of Chosun,
Gojong's Permission of Missions,
and Arrivals of Missionaries

Three Steps of Korean Missions

15 Religion

Chosun(the old name of Korea) understood Christianity as a vicious religion and strictly forbade Christianity. The early history of Catholic churches shows that a number of Catholics were persecuted under the government's ban. But Korea gradually opened its door to the world. In the process of the opening the Emperor permitted Christian missions, although they were limited, and missionaries officially entered the country.

In the period of opening, Korea first signed a treaty with Japan. On February 27, 1876, Korea signed the Korea-Japan Friendship Treaty on Gangwha Island. It included very unequal clauses despite of Korea's efforts. Under this treaty the Japanese could find an excuse to stay in Korea legally. Japan continuously forced Korea to sign other treaties such as Busan Port Settlement Treaty(January 30, 1877), Wonsan Port Opening Treaty(August 30, 1879) and Wonsan Port Settlement Treaty(August 4, 1881) that helped the Japanese expand their settlements in Korea.

On the other hand, the US mobilized a fleet and put pressure on Korea to open the country for strategic reasons and China intervened to restrain Japan from having an exclusive control over Korea. Under this external pressure Korea had to sign a treaty with the US. On May 22, 1882, the Korea-US Friendship Treaty clearly established a residential embassy in Seoul for the first time. Korea signed a treaty with China as well. On August 23, 1882, Korea signed the Korea-China Merchants Trading Agreement. With this treaty merchants other than diplomats could officially reside in Seoul.

After these early treaties Korea showed its intention to open the country through signing treaties consecutively with the UK, Germany, Italy, Russia, France, Austria, Hungary, Belgium and Denmark. These countries established their legations in Seoul. Diplomats, workers of diplomatic offices and merchants settled down in downtown Seoul, especially in the Chung-dong area. In this changing environment missionaries could find opportunities to enter Korea.

Korea opened its door to the world by making treaties with many countries in Asia and the world. Then Korea decided to send out diplomatic delegations to collect detailed information about other countries. One of the delegations was sent to the US. This delegation was assigned to deliver an official letter to the US President to formalize the diplomatic relationship between the two countries. It also had the duty to look at the political, cultural and social structures and systems in the US. Emperor Gojong selected Min Youngik as the head of the delegation and also included young intellectuals in their twenties.

The delegation to the US departed Jemulpo Port in July 1883 and arrived in San Francisco in September. They took a train to cross the continent and arrived in Washington, D.C. via Chicago and New York. On the train, they met J. F. Gaucher, a Methodist minister who was serving a church in Baltimore. Gaucher came to be interested in missions in Korea after this meeting. He donated funds to send missionaries to Korea. At the same time, he asked Robert S. Maclay, a famous Methodist missionary and a pioneer of missions in China and Japan, to visit Korea and examine the possibilities of missions there.

"Would you take some time and go to Korea to find a piece of land for the establishment of a mission department there? If this works we could be the first Protestant church to enter the land of strangers. If we can realize this plan it could be an honor to churches in Japan and you could add one

more to your achievements that you have contributed to our
church."

Maclay visited Korea for two weeks in response to Gaucher's request and the decision made by the global ministry of the US Methodist Church. He was helped by the pro-enlightenment politician Kim Okkyun and with whom he got acquainted during his stay in Japan. Thanks to his help, Maclay could deliver his letter stating his purpose of visit to Korea to Emperor Gojong. In the letter Maclay asked the Korean government to permit Christian missions.

A few days later Maclay met Kim Okkyun and heard the good news that Emperor Gojong had given permission to churches to begin hospitals and schools in Korea. This means that the Emperor of Korea officially permitted Christian missions on July 3, 1884. After getting the news, Maclay stayed in Seoul for a few more days and looked around Seoul and neighboring

▶ Jemulpo Port in 1886

areas. He already made a plan to set up a mission department in Chung-dong area where diplomatic offices were located.

In this changing environment, global ministry offices in the US began making detailed plans to send missionaries to Korea. The Presbyterian Church set up mission funds for Korea and selected missionaries, and the Methodist Church and the global ministry of the Methodist women's group also appointed missionaries in a hurry. In the meantime, Korea was getting ready to receive these missionaries.

The first missionary who officially settled down in Korea was H. N. Allen. He was a surgeon and was especially welcomed by diplomats who could not have medical treatments in Korea. They were therefore very friendly to Allen. With their help Allen could easily find a place for mission work. He could establish Jejung Hospital, the first modern hospital in Korea because he had happened to save the life of Min Youngik, a cousin of Empress Myungsung, thus gaining him the support of the Royal Family to the hospital. Jejung Hospital became a place for missionaries who came to Korea to stay, to prepare for and to have discussions about their missions in Korea. Missionaries such as Appenzeller and Underwood set up their mission offices in Chung-dong area and started activities helpful for their missions. Hospitals such as Jejung Women's Hospital, Si Hospital and Bogu Hosptial were established and schools such as Wonduwoo School, Baejae School and Ewha School were established with the big interest of the Royal Family. In 1887,

Saemoonan Church and Chungdong First Methodist Church were established. The opening of Korea, Emperor Gojong's permission to Christian missions, and the missionaries' arrivals proceeded in a smooth way.

Korea to the Western World

Influence of *The Korea Review* and *Korea Mission Field*

16 Religion

Korea has one of the most brilliant traditions in world history of pre-modern printing. A Buddhist printing made in the United Shilla Dynasty in the eighth century is recognized as the oldest wooden printing in the world. Korea used metal type for printing already in Koryo Dynasty and this was two centuries earlier than Gutenberg's printing in Germany. In spite of the legacy of inventing and developing printing skills much earlier than other countries, printing did not penetrate through Korean culture until the late nineteenth century. Ordinary people did not have much opportunity to read books. The modern printing history began with publishing books, newspapers, magazines and Christian materials in the era of opening the country.

The first modern printing business in Korea was Bakmoonggook, which was mostly run by the Japanese. Every publication was printed in Chinese. The first newspaper, *Hansung Newspaper* was published here. The first Korean private printing houses such as Gwanginsa and Hoedongseogwan started business before long.

The US Northern Methodist Church realized the importance of printing in Christian missions when public and private modern printing houses were opening in Korea. It installed printing machines in Baejae School and started printing Sammunsa in 1888. Sammunsa(The Trilingual Press) was the beginning of the Christian printing business in Korea.

Sammunsa was opened by Franklin Ohlinger in January 1892. It had the English name The Trilingual Press because in the house there were Korean, Chinese and English types and books and materials were printed in these three languages. This name meant that this printing house was supposed to transfer information and news in Chinese and English to Koreans and also news about Korea would be shared with the world. With this reason, Sammunsa published non-Christian books as well although it was run by a Christian organization. It was the most prominent printing house in Korea at that time.

Sammunsa expanded its business when S. A. Beck became director. He obtained 5,000 dollars of donations from American Christians in August 1900 and had the office equipped with a new bookbinding machine and new type. He also changed the name to Korea Methodist Publishing House.

There were many ways that missionaries shared information about their activities in Korea with people back home. Some missionaries wrote theses and some others published magazines. Among these the most famous publications were *The Korea Review* and *The Korean Mission Field*.

The Korea Review was an English monthly first published in 1901 by Homer B. Hulbert who took over the responsibility for Sammunsa from Ohlinger in September 1893. Hulbert edited *The Korean Repository* that published theses

HAPPY NEW YEAR

IX   JANUARY, 1913   No. 1

THE
KOREA MISSION
- FIELD -

THE WELLS MEMORIAL SCHOOL, SEOUL.

▶ The Korea Mission Field   KOREA

about Korean history, language and culture from 1895 to 1897. He passed the responsibility for Sammunsa to D. A. Bunker and began to teach at Hansung Teachers' School. *The Korean Repository* was reduced in size beginning in December 1898 and eventually stopped in June 1899. Hulbert published a new magazine that could share the news about Korea with the world in January

1901. This new magazine was *The Korea Review.*

The Korean Repository was published for seven years from January 1892 to December 1898 and *The Korean Review* for six years from 1901 to 1906. These two magazines introduced Korea's politics, economy, culture, custom, religion and language in detail to people abroad and therefore greatly contributed to enhancing people's understanding of Korean society.

The Korean Repository was the only English monthly magazine published in Korea after *The Korea Review.* Hulbert made clear the purpose of this magazine and the fields that it would deal with in the editorial of the first volume in 1901. He pointed out the need for an English magazine that could record the events in Korea. He wanted to collect and compare materials about Korean culture and present readers a space for sharing and exchanging information. He emphasized that the magazine would take responsibility for these tasks. The early volumes focused on these purposes and included study reports and news about Korean culture. The later volumes mainly included papers about Russia–Japan relations and Korea–Japan relations, especially after the Russia–Japan War in 1904. The magazine published the columns that strongly criticized Japan's attack on Korea after late 1905 and Japan recognized it as an anti-Japan behavior. The magazine eventually ended its publishing due to Japan's pressure.

The *Korea Mission Field* was published from November 1905 to November 1941. This English magazine was published based on the spirit of ecumenism. It integrated a quarterly magazine, *The Korea Field*, published by C. C. Vinton of the Presbyterian church and a monthly magazine, *The Korea Methodist* published by the Methodist church.

In its first volume, *The Korea Mission Field* mentioned that with its publication "a new age of unification for Christians and churches has begun." The Korea Council of Protestant Church Missions was responsible for this publication and the Christian Literature Society of Korea was in charge of printing.

The magazine was published monthly from 1905 to 1941 and included news about mission activities and a variety of issues in Korea. It therefore made a huge contribution to spreading news and information about Korea for a long time. In fact, one of main purposes of the magazine was to share information about Korea with readers other than providing news about mission activities. In the later years, it more often dealt with customs and historical events because many missionaries thought that one of their roles was to translate and introduce Korean culture to readers. They happily played this role and described the Korean style of life in detail and shared related stories even in the papers on mission activities.

In the early years, Wambold temporarily was

in charge of editing and increased the number of copies to 700 or 800. More than 1,000 people subscribed to the magazine after 1910. In the 1920s, it was recognized as one of the best publications in Korea compared to other newspapers and magazines in terms of its editing and contents.

The Korea Review and The Korea Mission Field obviously made a great contribution to changing the image of Korea that had been described as 'the land of morning calm,' 'a secluded country,' and 'a forbidden country' by Westerners. In addition, they contributed to sharing with the world Korea's unstable political situation in the twentieth century and to developing Korea's publishing culture.

Beginning of Korean Leadership
The First Korean Pastors

17 Religion

The first Korean pastor in the Korean Christian history is Kim Changsik who was ordained in the Methodist church. The training of Korean pastors began with the beginning of Christian missions in 1884–1885. Appenzeller opened a theology class at Baejae School and taught students after school hours. There was no faculty member and no classroom. He visited Pyongyang and Incheon, and invited Korean mission workers and opened intensive classes in the off-season of farming. Among those mission workers Kim Changsik and Kim Gibeom passed qualifying examinations and were ordained in the Korea Mission District meeting of the US

Northern Methodist Church held in Sangdong Church on May 14, 1901. Kim Changsik was older and ordained before Kim Gibeom in the meeting. This is why Kim Changsik is called the first Korean pastor.

Kim Changsik was a legendary mission worker in the early years of Christian missions in Korea. He was called 'Paul in Korea.' He was born in a poor farming family in 1857. He learned Chinese literacy in a village school and worked in the fields. At the age of fifteen he left hometown and travelled all over the country working as a farm servant, footman, porter and market trader. In 1886 at nineteen he got married Park Nodeok and settled down in the Namdaemoon(meaning south gate) area of Seoul.

At that time, there were horrific rumors in Seoul that Western missionaries abducted small children and killed them for eating. These rumors were made and spread by conservative anti-opening people who were against Christian missions. Kim Changsik also heard these rumors and wanted to witness missionaries' abduction of children himself. He intentionally got a servant job at the residence of Franklin Ohlinger, a Methodist missionary. He worked hard and got a promotion to work as a cook. He could watch Ohlinger's every move in the house. But he could not find any of the cruel behavior that he was expecting. He was rather deeply touched by the good characters and behaviors of the Ohlingers, and he opened his mind to Christianity. He eventually was baptized in

1890, after two years of working for the Ohlingers and became one of the mission workers officially assigned by the Department of Mission of the US Northern Methodist Church. He then went to Pyongyang with William. J. Hall, a medical missionary and engaged in mission work. Western missionaries could not work in public because Pyongyang was very conservative. Kim Changsik instead took the lead in buying a prostitute's house and building up the land for the missionary's residence, hospital, school and church.

In May 1894, the governor of Pyongyang Min Byungseok was against the opening of the country, and he sent ten Christians including Kim Changsik and other Methodists and Presbyterians who were helping missionaries to prison. He wanted to block the spread of Christianity in Pyongyang. He beat them, forced them to deny Christianity and asked for ransom. But Kim Changsik did not give in and was heavily beaten. He was almost dead. At the request of the missionaries, the US Legation strongly protested to the Korean government. By order of the Korean government Kim Changsik was freed after one week by the governor. The governor had to compensate the missionaries and he was fired before long.

In July 1894, Pyongyang became a battle field due to the China–Japan War. The churches and hospitals run by missionaries were recognized as extraterritorial areas and became shelters for civilians who could not escape. There was an epidemic after the war and Hall and Kim Changsik devoted themselves to taking care of patients without attending to themselves. As a result, Hall died of the epidemic and Pyongyang citizens were deeply touched by his sacrifice. This kind of sacrifice and devotion became the foundation of missions and contributed to making Pyongyang 'Jerusalem of Korea.'

Kim Changsik led Methodist meetings in the north of Pyongyang together with William A. Noble from 1896. He joined the Theology Gathering that began that year and took classes to be a pastor. From his ordination to retirement in 1924 he established 125 churches and constructed forty eight churches in Youngbyeon, Suwon and Haeju areas. He lived a dramatic life, changing social classes from being a servant to being the first Korean pastor. But he did not forget humbleness and obedience until the last minute of his life.

Kim Gibeom was born in Yeonan-gun, Hwanghae-do. It was not known when and why he came to Incheon. He got to know Christianity and became a Christian when he was living in Incheon by the introduction of No Byungil, a mission worker from Seoul.

The Presbyterian Church first ordained seven Korean pastors in a presbytery meeting held in Jangdaehyun Church in Pyongyang on September 17, 1907. They were Seo Kyungjo, Han Seokjin, Yang Jeonbaek, Bang Gichang, Gil Seonju, Lee Gipoong and Song Inseo who all had graduated from Pyongyang Theological Seminary in 1907.

Pyongyang Theological Seminary, the theological seminary of the Presbyterian Church of Korea, officially opened in 1903. But Bang Gichang and Kim Jongseop already started learning theology in Samuel A. Moffet's class in 1901 and Yang Jeonback, Gil Seonju, Lee Gipoong and Song Inseo joined this class in 1903. In 1904, fifteen others including Seo Kyungjo, Han Seokjin, Lee Wonmin and Choi Jongjin entered the seminary. Seo Kyungjo and Han Seokjin could be transferred to the third year thanks to their previous studies with missionaries. Therefore, there were eight in the third year. These students were granted diplomas at the first commencing ceremony held in Jangdaehyun Church on June 20, 1907.

The Presbyterian Church of Korea began with missionaries sent by the US Northern Presbyterian Church, Southern Presbyterian Church, Presbyterian Church of Australia

▶ First graduates of Pyongyang Theological Seminary

and Presbyterian Church in Canada. In 1901, the Korea council of Presbyterian churches was established and Korean Christians participated in this organization. But Koreans' voice and influence were very limited. As the day of ordination was approaching, missionaries raised a question about Korean pastors' affiliation. There were basically two options. One was to have them affiliated with the presbyteries back home and the other was to make them choose Korean presbyteries. But there could be many problems if Korean pastors were affiliated with the presbyteries back home. Missionaries finally decided to establish independent presbyteries in Korea and obtained permission from their home churches. They referred to the Presbyterian Church in India that had been recently established for the structure and to the Westminster Confession for political regulations. Through this process an independent presbytery of the Korean Presbyterian Church was established on September 17, 1907. Moffet was elected as the first chair of the presbytery and Han Seokjin as clerk and Song Inseo as vice-clerk. This independent presbytery had its first member pastors before long. The establishment of the independent presbytery in Korea was a meaningful event like the independence of the Presbyterian Church in Korea.

This independent presbytery decided to send a missionary in memory of the first ordination of pastors and sent Lee Gipoong to Jeju Island. Seo Kyungjo was a brother of Seo Sangryung who had started Sorae Church and was assigned to serve churches in Jangyeon, Ongjin and neighboring areas as a mission pastor. He also served Saemoonan Church with Underwood as a co-pastor from 1910. Gil Seonju was the first elder of Jaedeahyun Church and started dawn prayers for the first time in Korea and greatly contributed to the growth of churches in Pyongyang. He was assigned to serve Jangdaehyun Church after ordination. Bang Gichang was sent to Yonggang, Jejae and Judal churches as a mission pastor and Yang Jeonbaek to Suncheon, Jeongju and Pakchun churches also as a mission pastor. Han Seokjin was assigned to work for Pyongyang, Jangcheon, Mirim and Icheon churches as a mission pastor and Song Inseo for Jungsan, Hanchun, Oeseojang, Youngyu and Huhrimol churches as a mission pastor.

All the first Korean pastors to be ordained were sent to Pyongan-do and Hwanghae-do except for Lee Gipoong who was sent to Jeju. Gil Seonju was the only pastor in charge and all others were assigned to serve as mission pastors. These pastors were supposed to work with missionaries who took the general responsibility for the church. Mission pastors took care of selected areas under the order and supervision of missionaries. Their activities were limited but the existence of Korean pastors was the beginning of the Korean leadership in the Korean church.

The Spirit of Love Overcomes Hatred for Persecutors

History of Persecution

18 Religion

On March 13, 2009, a seminar on 'the restoration of Korean churches and the spirit of persecution' was held in Jonggyo Church in Seoul. Lee Deokju from the Methodist Theological Seminary made a presentation on the spirit of Rev. Joo Gicheol who had been persecuted. He emphasized that the real spirit of martyrdom was the spirit of love overcoming hatred for persecutors. According to him, martyrs often lived like martyrs even before external oppression and persecution resulted in their martyrdom. He continued that religious people who practiced 'white martyrdom' of tears and sweat in daily life could reach to 'red martyrdom' of blood at the last minute of their life.

This example of martyrdom is found in the case of Rev. Joo Gicheol who is considered one of the most prominent martyrs in the history of Korean churches. He refused to worship at Japanese shrines and was put in prison several times after 1938. He was severely tortured and died in prison in April 1944. He was repeatedly imprisoned because Japan oppressed him and repeatedly attempted to persuade him. But he never changed and he kept his faith. He could bear Japan's pressure, oppression, torture and imprisonment not by hatred for oppressors but by his love for Jesus Christ. He would say that "the absolute obedience only comes from love" and those who suffered could accept even martyrdom with pleasure not because they were pushed but because they were touched by the love of Jesus Christ. Rev. Joo admired those who suffered voluntarily with a happy mind and thought that this could only be possible with love.

There were already many martyrs even before

▶ A scene from the Jeamri massacre

the introduction of Protestantism to Korea. Lee Seonghoon, the first baptized Catholic was martyred with many other Catholics when the Shinyoo Persecution occurred in 1801. There were many others who tried to keep their faith even unto to death in the history of the Korean churches.

The first martyr in the history of Protestant churches was Rev. Robert Thomas. He was killed in relation to the General Sherman Incident* in 1866. Baek Hongjoon helped a missionary in China who was translating the bible into Korean. He worked as a mission worker and also a bible salesman and guide for missionaries. He was arrested in 1892 and tortured in prison. He was martyred in prison in 1893 and became the first Protestant Korean martyr. In 1910, many Christians who were engaged in the independence movement were arrested due to the 105 Incident. They were also imprisoned and tortured. Some of them and Rev. Jeon Deokgi died from the aftereffects of torture. In 1919, many Christians who participated in the March First Movement were arrested. Some Christians died in prison and most of them were from Jeamri Church in Suwon and Whasuri Church in Suchon.

The history of Korean churches' martyrdom can be divided in three periods. The first period is the 1930s. In

* General Sherman was a US trading vessel that wanted to trade with Chosun against the will of Koreans. General Sherman attacked, detained and looted the Koreans. After a week of confrontation and battle the vessel was set on fire by Chosun soldiers and all the crew died.

this period mission workers who had been sent to China were killed by Japanese soldiers and Korean communists in Manchuria. Missions in Manchuria began after Japan's colonization of Korea in 1910. Many Koreans who had been deprived of their lands after Japan's general land survey went to Manchuria to cultivate wild lands. Korean churches were very interested in missions to Koreans in Manchuria and sent missionaries and mission workers. This was the beginning of Korean missions in Manchuria.

Lloyd P. Henderson was engaged in missions to Koreans in Manchuria and was cruelly killed by the Japanese army in 1931. In 1935, Rev. Han Kyunghee, sent by the Presbyterian churches, was killed by communists. In the same period, Rev. Son Sangyeol who had been sent by the Donga Christian Church(now the Korean Baptist Church) was killed by the Japanese army and Rev. Kim Youngjin and Rev. Kim Youngkook were killed by communists in Jiandao. Kim Sangjoon, Ahn Seongchang, Lee Changhee, Yoo Younghak and Lee Hyungtae were killed by Japanese soldiers and communists in Manchuria. In Siberia, Rev. Kim Younghak, Kim Taedeok(a Methodist mission worker), Park Nogi, Kim Huiseo, Jeon Youngdae and Choi Ungseon from the Donga Christian Church were killed.

The second period of martyrdom was the late years of the Japanese colonialism. Many Christians refused to worship at Japanese shrines and kept their faith. Japan oppressed Koreans in this period more than before in order to assimilate them and to make Korea a base of military supplies for its planned wars in Asia and against the US. Japan made so-called a national ritual of worshipping at Japanese shrines and forced Koreans to join the ritual.

Missionaries understood it not as a simple national ritual but as a religious action of idolatry. In 1937, schools of the US Northern Presbyterian Church and Southern Presbyterian Church refused the ritual. Japan began arresting, imprisoning and torturing those who refused or opposed the ritual beginning in 1938. Choi Bongseok and Joo Gicheol from Presbyterian churches were martyred in prison and hundreds of Christians including ordained pastors Kim Seondoo, Lee Giseon, Chae Jeongmin, Go Heungbong, Han Sangdong, Joo Namseon, Son Yangwon and Yang Donggeun were imprisoned and tortured. Rev. Lee Younghan of the Methodist church was martyred in prison and Rev. Kang Jonggeun and Rev. Kwon Oenho were martyred in Seodaemoon Prison in Seoul and Choi Ingyu in a prison in Daejeon.

Baptist churches were especially damaged due to their emphasis on the Second Advent of Christ. In 1943, all pastors were imprisoned and Rev. Park Bongjin and Rev. Kim Yeon were martyred. Rev. Jeon Chigyu from the Donga Christian Church, Rev. Choi Taehyung from the Seventh-day Adventist Church, Rev. Huh Seongdo in Chungju, Rev. Choi Sangrim in Kyungnam-do, and Rev. Park Yeonsei and Kim Changok, an elder in Mokpo, were also martyred.

The third period of martyrdom was during the Korean War. In 1945, Korea was freed from the Japanese colonial rule but this joy did not last long enough. Korea experienced an extreme ideological confrontation between the north and the south. In the north, communists tried to establish a communist government and persecuted and martyred many Christians who supported democracy. In 1947, Rev. Lee Jeongsim were martyred and Kim Whasik, Ahn Seokjoon, Kim Hyungsoo, Kim Gilsoo, Kim Injoon, Kim Cheolhoon, Bae Deokyoung, Hyun Byungchan and Choi Taekgyu were martyred or disappeared.

In 1950, during the Korean War, more Christians were killed. Lee Seonghui, Shin Seokgu, Park Yoongryul, Seok Okrin, Moon Byungrok, Cho Seokhoon, Lee Jeongsoon, Oh Deoksam, Jeon Gichan and Kang Chooksoo were arrested and killed. During the War the number of martyrs

▶ Children picking wild greens after Jeamri Massacre

increased and Cho Huiryeom, Kwon Uibong, Park Kyunggoo, Kim Ikjoo, Han Sayeon, Kim Hongsik, Jeong Ilseon, Kim Uigeon, Cho Choonil, Kim Youngyoon, Kim Youngbeom, Kim Ikdoo, Seo Gihoon, Song Jeonggeun, Kang Unyoung, Kang Seongnam, Kim Insil, Byeon Cheonsik, Choi Gapeun and Kim Gwangbeom were killed. These were all ordained pastors.

In the south, Rev. Lee Dojong was killed during the April Third Incident on Jeju Island in 1948. In 1949, Huh Seongjae, an elder of Mosulpo Church, was killed by communists. Kim Byungjoon, Yoon Hyunggeun, Kim Changil and Rev. Son, Yangwon's two sons, Son Dongin and Son Dongshin were killed during the Yeosoon Incident.

In southern areas, ordained pastors Kim Joohyun, Kim Seongwon, Lee Jaegyu, Kim Jonghan, Ahn Deokyoon, Kim Byunggu, Kim Gyungyeop, Lim Jongheon, Won Changkwon, Kim Jongin and Kim Bango were killed. Lee Matae, Oh Byunggil, Lee Kwangnyeon, Park Bunggeun, Jeong Jaeryeon and Joo Samsil were all mission workers and were killed. Kim Soohyung, Bae Youngseok, Kim Jeongbok, Cho Sanghak, Son Yangwon, Park Seokhyun, Paek Namyong and Lee Yongeon were all ordained pastors and killed. Sixty six Christians were killed in Byungcheon Baptist Church in Nonsan and many other Christians of Wondang, Shingwan, Haeseong, Beopseongpo, Yeomsan, Yaweolri, Bokgil, Youngam, Gurim, Sangweol and Imja Churches were shot dead. In Seoul, many Christians were also killed including an elder named Kim Ungrak, and many ordained pastors including Namgoong Hyeok, Song Changgeun, Kim Yoosoon, Yang Joosam, Lee Geon, Park Hyeonmyung and Choi Daeyoung were kidnapped to the north and martyred. Other Christians who are not known and were also killed in the name of Jesus Christ.

Many Christians who were named above could be called martyrs or at the same time patriots because the line between the two was not clear. Lee Deokju explains that this is because religious and political protests were mixed at that time. This is the character of the history of martyrdom in Korean churches, which had religious motivations that were strongly influenced by political situations. Protestant churches' suffering and martyrdom originated from the political situations and motivations of the late Yi Dynasty and the Japanese colonial period and in many cases also began with the martyrdom of Catholics in the late Yi Dynasty. The resistance of Christians therefore was not only religious but also political and Christians very often became scapegoats of political oppression. Japan accused Christians who refused to worship at Japanese shrines for purely religious motivations as anti-government political offenders and tried them under security and pubic order laws. The martyrdom of Christians during the Japanese colonial era could therefore be seen to include nationalistic resistance and patriotism, according to Lee Deokju.

Leadership in Democratization, Human Rights and Reunification Movements
Korea National Christian Council

The churches introduced to Korea were denominationally divided by different theological backgrounds and doctrines. In 1905, four mission departments of Presbyterian churches and two mission departments of Methodist churches united and organized the General Council of Protestant Evangelical Missions in Korea. The goal of this council was to work together for missions and ultimately to found one united Protestant church in Korea. Missionaries actively supported this idea but the idea was not realized because of different denominational interests.

On September 24, 1924, the Korean National Christian Council was founded in Saemoonan Church. This was the representative church organization that brought together the Federal Council of Protestant Missions and the Korean Church Federal Council. Rev. Cha Jaemyung was elected as the first president of the council. The founding assembly made clear the purposes of the council: 1. collaborate and spread the gospel; 2. collaborate and promote social morality; 3. collaborate and spread Christian culture.

The Presbyterian Church and the Methodist Church participated in the foundation assembly and six mission departments of the US, Australian and Canadian churches also participated. The Korean Bible Society and the YMCA participated as Christian organizations. Eleven churches and organizations were the first members of this council that is now the National Council of Churches in Korea(NCCK). However, it changed to the Korea National Church Council in 1931 and dissolved in 1937.

On the other hand, Korean churches participated in world ecumenical meetings since the early twentieth century. Yoon Chiho participated in the World Missionary Conference held in Edinburgh in 1910. This conference became the International Missionary Council afterward. In the changing world situation, the Korea National Christian Council became a national ecumenical organization affiliated with the International Missionary Council.

Korean representatives outnumbered missionaries in the Korea National Christian Council because of membership regulations. It was possible for Koreans to lead the council. Then missionaries reversed the previous decision to dissolve the Federal Council of Protestant Missions. They maintained this council and at the same time, participated in a limited way in the Korea National Christian Council that was led by Koreans. Koreans could participate in mission programs that had been led by missionaries. This change greatly contributed to overcoming Koreans' dependency on missionaries and to the building of Korean churches by Koreans. But the Korea National Christian Council was closed in the late years of the Japanese colonial rule and the Korea National Church Council, a pro-Japan organization, was founded soon afterward. The Korean churches were integrated into the Korean Church of Japan Christian Church in 1945.

The reconstruction of the nation and the churches began after the independence of the country. The Korean Church of Japan Christian Church was dissolved and the Chosun Christian Council was founded in the fall of 1946. This council changed its name to the Korea Christian Council after the establishment of the Korean government. The Korea Christian Council sent a representative to the founding assembly of the WCC in Amsterdam in August 1948 and participated in the world ecumenical movement. The Korea Christian Council suffered with the rest of the country from the Korean War and the divide of Korea and made efforts to deal with national problems domestically and internationally.

In 1961, the International Missionary Council was integrated into the WCC and became one of the branch organizations of the WCC. This change was based on the premise that missions and churches could not be separated and that churches must lead the broad area of missions. In this changing world environment, the Korea Christian Council changed to the National Council of Churches in Korea(NCCK) and its membership was limited to denominations. The character of the council changed from a Christian council to a church council. The NCCK took on national mission agendas of human rights, democratization and reunification.

The NCCK led the Christian democratization movement. After independence, churches cooperated with the Rhee Syngman government without repenting their wrong doing under the Japanese colonial rule including worshipping at Japanese shrines. Churches had an opportunity to reflect on their ignorance of their prophetic duties after the April 19 Revolution in 1960* but they lost this opportunity. Churches supported the May 16 Coup in 1961.** Christian youth first joined political demonstrations to protest against the Korea-Japan Summit for

---

* The April 19 Revolution was led by students who strongly protested against the Rhee Syngman government's election malpractice. President Rhee Syngman eventually resigned.

** This was a military coup led by Park Chunghee. This was the beginning of his eighteen years of dictatorship.

the restoration of diplomatic relations. Churches were divided into two, those supporting and those opposing the constitutional amendment of the Park Chunghee government.* Park Chunghee declared a state of emergency and martial law in 1971. He amended the constitution and made the Yushin Constitution in 1972 that strengthened his control, extended his dictatorship and weakened the power of Congress.

The Park Chunghee government repressed protests against the Yushin Constitution and regarded them as internal disturbances. One example of this oppression was the Mincheonghakryun Incident that the government fabricated to repress protests in April 1974. 1,024 people were investigated and 183 of them were sentenced to imprisonment including some with death penalties and life sentences. Member denominations of the NCCK and individual churches strongly protested against the unjust trials and sentences. They began the 'Thursday Prayer' on July 11, 1974, bringing together young pastors, prisoners' families and lay people. Additionally, the NCCK launched the Human Rights Committee on May 4, 1974 and began protecting and promoting human rights in Korean society. Youth representatives of the NCCK member denominations founded the Ecumenical Youth Council in Korea(EYCK) in January 1976. EYCK played a leading role in the Christian democratization movement from the late 1970s to the 1980s.

* Park Chunghee amended the constitution to make his third term legal in 1969.

In May 1975, the 9th state of emergency began and it lasted until October 26, 1979. The NCCK revived the Thursday Prayer on January 15, 1976 and this prayer meeting became a symbolic protest under Park Chunghee's authoritarian Yushin government. The Park Chunghee government manipulated big Christian gatherings to show the world that Koreans were enjoying the freedom of religion. Billy Graham's Korea Mission Gathering, and CCC's Explo 74 and 77 Gatherings for National Evangelization were all supported by the government. Conservative Christians who were supported by the government criticized the democratization movement and activities as communist campaigns. They maintained a close relationship with the government and expanded their influence. They provided the government with strong political support throughout the dictatorship. Park Chunghee's dictatorship ended with his death in 1979. In May 1980 the Gwangju Massacre occurred and Chun Doohwan's dictatorship began. The NCCK protested against the harsh political oppression and organized and led diverse activities and programs for democratization and human rights.

The NCCK also led the reunification movement of the Korean churches. The discussion on reunification had been in stalemate since the 1970s. It was simply difficult to deal with reunification issues because of the government's interference. But the NCCK decided to have a special committee that could study and discuss reunification issues in February 1982. The government strongly suppressed the NCCK's reunification programs until March 1985. But the 34th General Assembly of the NCCK in March 1985 adopted the Korean Churches' Statement on Peace and Reunification. This was the beginning of the NCCK's reunification movement.

The Korean Churches' Statement on Peace and Reunification of the Korean Peninsula(the so-called 88 Statement) was adopted by the 37th General Assembly on February 29, 1988. This statement of NCCK member denominations showed the Christians' strong will for peace and for the reunification of the two Koreas to the nation and the world. It included the churches' discussions on reunification and also the successful results of reunification activities. It was a historical statement with important reflection on the churches' reunification discussions and presentation of the new direction of the churches' reunification movement. This statement made a great contribution to promoting discussions on reunification not only in the churches but in Korean society as well.

Nation

Christians' Efforts for Independent Democracy and their Ordeals

The 105 Incident and Shinminhoe

20 Nation

Japan officially colonized Korea in 1910 and set up strategies to occupy Korea permanently. Japan carried out a general land survey across the country to make the transfer of estates to the Japanese easy and manipulated different procedures to disturb and obtain social properties. Japan also tried to dissolve the organizations that were expressing any support to Korea's independence and to eliminate the individuals who were leading the independence movement. Japan especially watched over many Christians with suspicion. In October 1909, Ito Hirobumi, Japan's Resident-General in Korea was assassinated by An Junggeun at Harbin Railway Station in

China. Japan colonized Korea after this event and Terauchi Masadake was assigned to be the first Governor-General of Korea.

In December 1910, Japan fabricated a story that Korean Christians tried to assassinate Terauchi while he on his way to Sinuiju to participate in the completion ceremony of the Aprok iron bridge. This was the so-called 105 Incident because 105 people were sent to prison by decision of the court. In 1905, Japan forced Korea to sign on to the Ulsa Agreement* and forced Emperor Gojong to give up the throne in 1907. Japan then imposed a security law on Koreans. Japan dissolved most organizations by announcing a private school law in 1908, a publishing law in 1909 and a ban on assembly and demonstration in 1910. But Japan could not dissolve churches and Christian schools that were considered to be relatively open-minded.

Then Anak Incident occurred in 1910. Japan arrested 160 patriotic Christians in Hwanghae-do during this incident. They were raising funds to establish a military school in Manchuria, China. This school was planned by An Myunggeun, a cousin of An Junggeun. In 1911, Japan arrested Christian students who organized Haryeonghoe and were active in educating students and youth groups about the need for Korea's independence. After colonizing Korea, Japan was not comfortable with the YMCA's activities and even its existence. Japan

* Japan deprived Korea of diplomatic rights according to this agreement.

continued arresting students and accusing them falsely until the number reached 700. The false accusation was that many Christians hid handguns and tried to kill Terauchi when he was going to the completion ceremony of the Aprok iron bridge. Terauchi's train did not stop and they said the Christians then tried to kill him again when he was meeting McQueen, a missionary in Seonchun, after the ceremony. But the police were on high alert and Christians failed again, according to the accusation.

Lee Seunghoon, An Taeguk, Yang Gitak, Lim Chijeong and Yoo Dongryeol were arrested and lecturers of Haryeonghoe such as Yoon Chiho, Yang Jeonbaek and Yang Joonmyung were also arrested. These people were severely tortured. They were beaten by long bamboo spears and tortured until all fingernails and toenails were removed in the winter time. At last, the torturers were exhausted and made the prisoners fast for four days. Nothing was given to the prisoners, not even water, and nobody answered to their entreaties for water. Kim Geunhyung and Jeong Heesoon died from this cruel torture.

Arrested Christians refused to sign false confession papers. In March 1912, the tortures ended and seven leaders and 120 conspirators were sent to the court based on false confession papers they had signed. But they strongly resisted in the court. Yoon Chiho made clear that their confessions were all false and Yang Gitak and Yoo Dongryeol also asserted their innocence. All the evidences presented in the court showed that the indictment itself was groundless. But the court only freed seventeen and declared 105 guilty in October 1912. The name '105 Incident' was from this number of prisoners.

Eighteen including Ok Gwanbin were sentenced to seven years, thirty nine including Lee Deokwhan to six years and forty two including Oh Daeyoung to five years of imprisonment. All of them resisted the ruling and appealed to the Higher Court. In the second trial ninety nine were found not guilty and freed. Six of them(Yang Gitak, An Taeguk, Lee Seonghoon, Lim Chijeong, Yoon Chiho and Ok Gwanbin) were sentenced to four years of imprisonment.

Japan clearly showed its intention in the 105 incident to oppress Christians and continue its colonial rule in Korea. Japan also pointed out missionaries such as McQueen, Moffet, Roberts and Sharrocks as puppet masters behind the incident and falsely accused them of agitating Korean Christians and telling them to be prepared for the next opportunity of assassination. Missionaries strongly denied Japan's accusation against them and against others, and they asked Terauchi to reinvestigate the incident from the beginning. They also shared the news about the suffering and imprisonment of innocent Koreans including Yoon Chiho, the vice-chair of YMCA for relations to Christian organizations abroad.

Philip L. Gillett revealed the false accusation

of Japan that Christian students in the Christian group Haryeonghoe had tried to assassinate Terauchi. He also revealed that Japan indicted innocent Christians based on forced confessions after severe tortures. Gillett was expelled due to this revelation. He then worked with YMCA China and continued supporting Koreans' independence movement.

The 105 Incident was Japan's plot to dissolve the YMCA and eventually Shinminhoe. Japan was especially concerned about Shinminhoe, a secret patriotic organization. This organization was started by An Changho in February 1907 when churches were rapidly growing. The root of the organization was Sangdong Youth School in Sangong Church that was begun by Jeon Deokgi. An Cangho wanted to establish a patriotic organization bringing Christian young people in the northwest area together. The platforms of Shinminheo were to promote national pride and independent spirit, to build national power for independence, to establish educational institutions promoting youth education, to eliminate corrupted ideas and customs through promoting diverse industries and to build a free, civilized country through empowering people.

Shinminhoe had positions such as general secretary, general clerk, finance officer and administrative officer. The central committee was the highest decision making body. The organization was based on secret cells that no more than two persons could have any direct contact with and therefore, they could not know each other. It organized overseas as well as domestic networks. Newly educated intellectuals, merchants, Christian nationalists from the northwest area, members of Sangdong Church, overseas educated nationalists, high class politicians and former government officials were the main members in the organization. Shinminhoe was a predominantly-Christian anti-Japan organization.

There were two major groups in Shinminhoe. One was led by An Changho and moderate reformers joined this group. The other was led by Lee Donghui and more inclined to support armed resistance. The group led by An Changho emphasized the enlightenment and empowerment of people and therefore focused on education and national industries. But Japan officially colonized Korea in 1910 and the group that was led by Lee Donghui and inclined to armed resistance obtained more support and power. Ideas about strong anti-Japan resistance movement such as the assassination of pro-Japan figures and the establishment of a military school were supported by members of Shinminhoe and An Changho's empowerment strategy gradually lost support and power.

During these changes within Shinminhoe, the 105 Incident occurred in 1911 and Shinminhoe was gradually revealed to the public. In fact, Japan came to know the existence of Shinminhoe through the Anak incident in 1910. Japan therefore fabricated the 105 Incident and cruelly tortured those who were arrested to get detailed information about Shinminhoe. Japan eventually found that fifty-seven out of the 123 arrested were members of Shinminhoe. But the organization was operated in secret and members did not know one another. Japan could not have any more information.

Japan wanted the 105 Incident to bring about the dissolution of Shinminhoe but instead the spirit of Shinminhoe was strengthened. The idea of establishing an independent national democracy was passed on to the next generation and inherited by the March First Movement in 1919. It also became a spiritual and ideological foundation for the interim government based in Shanghai. In 1948 after independence from Japan, Korea established a republic and enacted its first constitution that could be the foundation of society. The spirit of the first constitution originated from Shinminhoe's ideas. Christians in the independence movement developed Shinminhoe's ideas of a new nation and these ideas contributed to the establishment of a modern country after independence.

Contributions to the Independence Movement
and the Establishment of an Interim Government

The March First Movement
and Korean Churches

21 Nation

The March First Movement was an
unprecedented event in the history of Korea's independence
movement: the entire nation and all classes of society
participated. This movement was recognized by the world as a
notable non-violent civil action. Many Christians played
important roles in the movement.

Background and preparation of the March First Movement

The background of the movement was Japan's

occupation and oppressive colonial rule of Korea. Japan officially colonized Korea with the Japan-Korea Annexation Treaty in 1910. Koreans could not accept the new reality and strongly protested against Japan's occupation. Japan established the military police and severely oppressed Koreans. Most Koreans could not find enough food and daily necessities because Japan took almost everything. Japanese goods were imported and Japanese investors came to Korea. Korean industries were occupied by the Japanese and could not be developed. Koreans suffered economically and starved every day. Japan tried to assimilate Korea and thereby to get rid of almost everything Korean including educational institutes, ideologies and religions. Japan wanted to destroy Korea's spirit and culture. But Japan's oppressive religious policies actually were a stimulus to religious people. Churches and other religious groups led the March First Movement because religious institutions were the only legal entities at that time and above all, religious people were very angry about Japan's oppression of religions.

In the 1910s, people built up their capacity for an independence movement inside and outside the country. It was not possible to establish legal organizations in Korea and many groups acted in secret. In particular, Chosunkukminhoe, Giseongboldan and Songjookhoe were all underground groups organized by Christians in northwest area. Christians in this area also actively participated in Shinminhoe, an underground group in the past. Sinminhoe was revealed to the public during the 105 Incident. Some intellectuals who were living in exile overseas worked with others in Korea to prepare an armed independence struggle. They were also engaged in diplomatic activities revealing Japan's oppression to the press and sharing Koreans' suffering with people. These independence activists made efforts to strengthen the capacity of the independence movement and waited for the right time to restore the sovereignty of the Korean people.

The first opportunity came when the First World War was ending. The world political environment was changing with US President Woodrow Wilson's assertion of 'the principle of the self-determination of peoples' and the Paris Peace Conference. Shinhan Youth Group in Shanghai sent Kim Gyusik, an elder of Saemoonan Church to the Peace Conference. This became the stimulus for the March First Movement. Kim Gyusik said before his departure "…nobody would know which country I am from. Somebody in Korea must proclaim Korea's independence so that I can reveal Japan's oppression. Something must happen in Korea so that I can do my work in Paris." He asked his colleagues to organize demonstrations in Korea. In response to his request, Yeo Unhyung went to China and announced the Muo Independence Statement on February 1, 1919 together with activists in Manchuria, Siberia and the US.

Meanwhile, Lee Gyusik who was studying in Japan returned from Shanghai to Tokyo and shared the information about Kim Gyusik's participation in the Peace Conference with his colleagues. At that time the Korean YMCA office in Tokyo was the meeting place of Korean students. They discussed Wilson's idea of people's self-determination and the independence movement by Koreans in the US, and were encouraged very much. They organized an independence movement group and prepared a statement on Korea's independence. On February 8, 1919, they gathered in the Korean YMCA office, announced the statement and sent it to the Japanese government, its ministers, the congress and the press. This was the February 8 Independence Statement.

In Korea, leaders of Chondogyo, an indigenous religion, Christianity and Buddhism organized an association. Seonwoo Hyuk from Shanghai met Christian leaders in the northwest area and shared the information about Kim Gyusik's participation in the Peace Conference. The Christian leaders were encouraged by this news and Lee Seunghoon designed action plans for Christians in the northwest area and Seoul. Additionally, leaders of Chondogyo heard the news about the February 8 Independence Statement from Song Gyebaek who had participated in the Tokyo meeting which made the statement. They began preparing an independence campaign. The leaders of Christianity and Chondogyo separately prepared action plans at the same time. They noticed each other's plans and sought a joint course of action. Leaders of Chondogyo, Christianity and Buddhism agreed it was time to organize a national association. Christian leaders headed up the organizing of religious leaders and preparations for the March First Movement. Forty eight national leaders jointly prepared the Independence Statement of the March First Movement and twenty three of the thirty three signatures were from Christian leaders.

The March First Movement

On March 1, 1919, more than 1,000 students and citizens gathered at Pagoda Park in Jongno, Seoul. Jeong Jaeyong from Kyungshin School went up to the octagonal bower and read the Independence Statement starting with "We Koreans now proclaim that Korea is an independent country and that the Korean nation is a self-determined people." Twenty nine national leaders out of the thirty three who had signed the statement gathered at Taewhagwan restaurant near Pagoda Park and announced the statement. Choi Namseon drafted the statement and Lee Gwangsoo edited it. Han Yongwoon added three public commitments to the statement. The students and citizens at Pagoda Park ran out into the Jongno streets holding national flags and shouting 'Independence for Korea!' Ten years of silence was broken and the people's outcry spread across the country.

Christian leaders took important roles in the March First Movement, including participating in people's actions across the country, establishing the interim government in Shanghai, China and organizing the overseas independence movement. First of all, they led the March First Movement. People's gatherings on March 1 were organized in many cities such as Seoul, Pyongyang, Seonchun, Uiju and Wonsan. In

Pyongyang, Christians from six churches and Christian students gathered at Soongdeuk School, a Christian school under the leadership of Rev. Gil Seonjoo of Jangdaehyun Church and Rev. Shin Heungsik of Namsanhyun Church(two of the thirty three national leaders). Rev. Kim Seondoo of Seomoonbak Church led the gathering and Jeong Ilseon, a mission worker of Seomoonbak Church, read the independence statement. Rev. Gang Kyuchan of Sanjeonghyun Church made a speech and Rev. Do Inkwon and elder Yoo Wonsam led the people's demonstration. In Jinnampo, Pyongyang, 500 students, Christians and other citizens gathered at Shinheung Methodist Church and participated in a street demonstration. Rev. Shin Heungsik and Hong Giwhang, the headmaster of Samsoong Christian School, led the gathering. Rev. Yang Jeonbaek(one of the thirty three national leaders) and Kim Jiwoong, a teacher at Shinseong School, led the public gathering and demonstration. 600 citizens and Christians including 150 students from Shinseong Church participated in the gathering. Hong Seungik read the independence statement and Jeong Sangin led the people's demonstration, both were teachers at Shinseong School. Rev. Yoo Yeodae(one of the thirty three national leaders) led a public demonstration with hundreds of participants in Uiju, Pyonganbuk-do. In Wonsan, Hamkyungnam-do, Rev. Jeong Choonsu(one of thirty three national leaders), Gwak Myungil, a mission worker, and Lee Gasoon, another Christian, led a public gathering. Christians also organized and led public gatherings and demonstrations in Gaesung, Hamheung and Sariwon. These gatherings contributed to spreading people's actions and demonstrations across the country.

          According to the statistics of the Japanese Government-General, although they are hard to fully trust, there were 848 demonstrations in March and 600,000 people participated in these demonstrations. According to Park Eunsik's 'History of Korean Independence Movement(1920)', there were more than 1,500 demonstrations from March to May with more than 2 million participants. Many Christians actively participated in demonstrations. According to the statistics on the March First Movement(from March 1 to May 27), 22 percent of those who were indicted for involvement were Christians(1,719 people) and 15 percent were Chodongyo believers(1,207 people). The number of the convicted(between March 1 and May 30, 1919) was 9,059, including 2,032 Christians(22.4 percent) and 1,363 Chondogyo believers(15 percent). At that time the whole Christian population was about 290,000, only 1.8 percent of the total population, which was then 16 million. The number of Chondogyo believers was about one million. This shows that Christians participated in the March First Movement in the most active way.

          The main reason why the March First Movement spread so quickly to the entire country was that statements, posters and underground newspapers had been rapidly distributed across the country. The press was severely oppressed at that time. Most newspapers and magazines published by Koreans were banned. Only the Japanese Government-General's official newspapers and Japanese magazines could be legally published. The newspapers published abroad by Koreans could not be brought to Korea. In particular, Japan tightly controlled and inspected all telegraphs and communications in Korea and the newspapers published in Japan. In this situation, the distribution of statements and underground newspapers with the news about people's demonstrations on March 1 in major cities greatly contributed to the spread of the March First Movement to the whole country. Christians especially worked hard to copy and distribute statements, posters and underground newspapers under Japan's tight surveillance. This was one of the most important roles that Christians played in the March First Movement.

Japan oppressed Christians in a cruel way after the March First Movement. One of the cruelest examples was the Jeamri Church Massacre when Japan set fire to the church and killed the Christians inside. Japan oppressed Christians all over the country. The Japanese military police would intrude into churches and beat and arrest Christians who were participating in the prayer meetings that had been reported to the police. The police also would inspect people on the street and beat and arrest Christians. Non-Christians, however, were easily freed. In case of Yuldu in Pyongananm-do, the Japanese military police threatened and instigated villagers to oust Christians from the village. As a result, Christians had to escape to the mountains. According to a report of the PCK(Presbyterian Church of Korea) General Assembly in 1919, twelve PCK churches and eight schools were destroyed. Forty one church members were killed and six were beaten to death. 3,804 were arrested and 134 out of them were church leaders, including pastors and elders. This number represents 13 percent of all the leaders.

Christians were actively engaged in the establishment of the interim government that was the foundation of the long-term independence movement in Korea. After the March First Movement pastors including Kim Byungjo, Hyun Soon, Son Jeongdo, Lee Wonik and Kim Injeon, and other Christians including Seo Byungho, Jeong In, Jo Sangseop and Yeo Unhong sought refuge in Shanghai. They led the establishment of the interim government. Christians inside Korea also participated in establishing the interim government. One of the prominent figures was Lee Gyugap. He was sent to Shanghai as the representative of the Hanseong(old name of Seoul) Interim Government and worked to integrate the two interim governments in Seoul and Shanghai. As a result, the interim government in Shanghai could have the legitimate status to represent all Koreans inside and outside Korea.

Meanwhile, Christians formed underground groups among the members who joined the movement. The main purpose of these groups was to keep in contact with the interim government in Shanghai and to deliver the funds raised in Korea. Christians in Pyongyang including Park Seungmyung, Kim Seongtak, Park Ingwan, Go Jinhan and Park Jeongik formed the Korean People's Organization. They secretly contacted the interim government in Shanghai and made branches in other major cities. The Korean Youth Independence Organization was also formed in Pyongyang with the leadership of Rev. Jeong Jinhyun who had led a demonstration in Kangseo-gun, Pyongannam-do and escaped to Shanghai. He later returned to Korea as an officer of the interim government and organized a branch of the interim government with Hwangbo Deoksam, a student of the Pyongyang Theological Seminary. He would receive messages from Shanghai and deliver them to underground groups in Korea, and he sent the news about the Korean situation to Shanghai. He also formed the Korean Youth Independence Organization together with An Youngsik, Park Jongeun and Park Seonju who were all Methodist mission workers. This organization was engaged in underground publishing and fundraising, and they led demonstrations.

Jo Mansik, an elder and the headmaster of Osan School, was responsible for building a secret communication channel between Seoul and Andong, China. He worked with Christian colleagues like Kim Byungtak, Lee Jeongchan and Choi Youngman. The communication between Seoul and Andong was very dangerous. He opened a furniture shop in Seoul and would send messages and funds together with furniture to Andong. He also organized a musical band and performed in cities for fundraising.

Christians also played an important role in reaching out to the international press. This activity was especially carried out by Koreans abroad. One good example was the Shanghai Korean Church's activity. This church was located in a foreign concession and could easily escape from Japan's interference. This church had a close relationship with the interim government nearby. Many Christians who sought in refuge in Shanghai came to this church regardless of their denominations. These Christians shared information with missionaries about the Korean independence movement and Japan's oppression, and reached out to the international press. They also sent letters to US churches and politicians and revealed Japan's oppression and persecution of Christians and shared the Koreans' strong will for independence. As a result of this effort, they received supporting messages from eighteen US congressmen.

Christians in the US actively participated in independence movement as well. Ahn Changho who was staying in San Francisco first heard the news about the March First Movement from Rev. Hyun Soon in Shanghai. He shared this news with Rhee Syngman, Jeong Hankyung and Seo Jaepil. The central committee of the Korean People's Organization in the US decided to send Rhee Syngman and Jeong Hankyung to Paris, and to contact US political, religious and social organizations to share about the Korean independence movement. Additionally, Ahn Changho went to Shanghai in early April as the representative of Koreans in the US to assist the establishment of the interim government.

Seo Jaepil organized the Korea Freedom Day

in Philadelphia in mid-April. Koreans and 150 American pastors and professors who were supporting Korea's independence joined the Korea Freedom Day ceremony. Seo Jaepil revealed Japan's cruel oppression and shared about the Koreans' strong will for independence with Americans. He then founded the Korea Information Bureau and published materials to share the news about Korea with Western countries. He also organized the League of the Friends of Korea, inviting pastors, intellectuals and politicians to join, and made efforts to gain their attention and support for Korea.

As the result of these efforts, *The Korean Situation* was published in the summer of 1919 by the National Council of the Churches of Christ in the USA. This report revealed Japan's suppression of the Koreans' independence movement and Japan's persecution of Christians. It caught the attention of churches and ordinary people in the US, and finally the US Congress began discussing Korean matters. *The Korean Situation* was printed in the Congressional record and Homer B. Hulbert, who had worked in Korea as a missionary, was called in to give a testimony about Korea and its history to the Congress. Hulbert pointed out the US government's ignorance of Japan's occupation of Korea although the US had signed the US-Korea Friendship Treaty in 1882 and acknowledged then the responsibility to assist Korea. He explained that the Korea-Japan Agreement in 1905 was illegal because it had not gained Emperor Gojong's permission and the Japan-Korea Annexation Agreement in 1910 was also illegal. He argued that Japan's occupation of

▶ The international press described the March First Movement as a non-violent resistance

Korea was therefore illegal. In response to Hulbert's testimony, Senators C. S. Thomas and S. P. Spencer presented a motion supporting Korea's independence to the Congress. This motion was rejected but the motion itself was the result of Koreans' hard efforts and therefore, it encouraged Koreans in the US.

The March First Movement and Christian Women's Role

Christian women had an enormous role in the March First Movement but their role was not properly acknowledged. They played an important role in preparing the March First Movement, organizing demonstrations and establishing the interim government.

In the preparation of the March First Movement, Kim Soonae(Kim Gyusik's wife) came to Korea with Sunwoo Hyun carrying a secret letter from the Shanghai Korean

Youth Organization. She shared the information about Koreans' activities in Shanghai and encouraged people to join the independence movement in Korea. Her activities contributed to Christians' participation in independence demonstrations in Seoul. Kim Maria who was the representative of the Tokyo Women's Fellowship provided the Korean Youth Organization for Independence with funding and contributed to the announcement of the February 8 Independence Statement. She came to Korea with Hwang Esther to share the detailed information about the statement. These two women met Park Indeok, Shin Joonryeo and Kim Whallan who were teaching at Ewha School, and Son Jeongsoon, Na Hyeseok, Ahn Sookja and Ahn Byungsook who were students and graduates of Ewha School. They shared about the independence activities in Shanghai and Tokyo. They decided to organize a women's group for the independence movement and suggested that students of Christian girls' schools such as Ewha, Chungshin and Baewha suspend their participation in classes. Kim Maria and Hwang Esther were arrested immediately after the March First Movement.

Female Christian students were separately in contact with the YMCA group which was secretly participating in the preparation of the March First Movement. In particular, Ewha School was used as the focal point for female students' meetings and communication, and for copying and distributing statements and materials. On March 1, students of Ewha School, Chungshin Girls' School and Baewha Girls' School led demonstrations, though of a smaller size. Other women also participated in the demonstrations. Ten nurses of the Severance Hospital participated in the demonstration on March 6 carrying medical supplies to take care of wounded people.

The Japanese Government–General closed the schools in Seoul as the number of students participating in demonstrations was increasing. Japan expected that students from local cities would return to their hometowns and that demonstrations would naturally decrease. But female students who had led demonstrations in Seoul actively shared the information about the March First Movement and organized and led demonstrations in their hometowns. Ewha School student Ryu Gwansoon returned to her hometown of Aune in Cheonan after the closing of the school. She shared the information about the March First Movement with her father and members of Maebong Church. She persuaded people and suggested to organize a demonstration in Cheonan. On April 1, a demonstration took place in Aune Market and she led the demonstration. She was only sixteen years old then. She was arrested and imprisoned in Seodaemoon Prison. She was tortured in a cruel way and died in prison.

The demonstrations organized and led by Christian women and female students took place all over the country. Lee Kyungji and Lee Kyungchae, sisters and students of Holston Girls' School in Gaesung were encouraged by Ahn Byungsook to organize a demonstration. They met Uh Yoonhee, a female mission worker of Choonggyo Church, and gained her agreement. Uh Yoonhee suggested other female mission workers to join and prepared a demonstration. On March 3, Christian women including students of Holston Girls' School ran out to the street and demonstrated, singing together Chanmiga, a hymn and Doknipga, a song about independence. Citizens of Gaesung joined this demonstration and the number of participants increased up to 2,000. They demonstrated until late night.

In Busan, Joo Kyungae, a teacher of Ilshin Girls' School discussed a demonstration with other teachers on March 10. They made national flags and led a demonstration the next day. Many students and members of Busanjin Church participated in the demonstration. This demonstration was connected with demonstrations on April 3 and 8, and contributed to the spread of demonstrations in Busan and Kyungsangnam-do areas. In Jinju, nurses of Baedon Hospital(a Christian hospital) led a demonstration with students of Gwanglim School(a Christian school). Many citizens in the market joined this demonstration and the number of participants reached to 2,000. The staff of Baedon Hospital treated wounded people. Many students of Soongui Girls' School in Pyongyang, Shinmyung Girls' School in Daegu, Chungmyung Girls' School in Mokpo, Gijeon Girls' School in Jeonju and Speer Girls' School in Gwangju played a very important role in organizing and leading demonstrations all over the country. In addition, Christian women and female students engaged in copying and distributing independence statements and delivering messages. They also persuaded and encouraged people to organize and participate in demonstrations.

Christian women were involved in the establishment of the interim government in direct and indirect ways. The alumni of Chungshin Girls' School organized the Patriotic Women's Organization in April with the suggestion of Oh Hyunjoo and the agreement of Oh Hyungwan, Lee Jeongsook, Jang Seonhee and Lee Seongwan. At this time, Kim Wonkyung, Choi Sookja and Lim Duksan also organized the Korea Patriotic Women for Independence. These two groups integrated according to the request of the interim government in Shanghai and had a new name, Korea Patriotic Women's Organization. This organization established branches in major cities such as Daegu and Busan. It raised funds from its members and sent the funds to the interim government.

Kim Maria and Hwang Esther were freed when demonstrations were suspended. The Korean Patriotic Women's Organization decided to elect new officers and rearrange the organization. Kim Maria was elected as the president, Lee Hyekyung as the vice president and Hwang Esther as the general secretary. Under the new leadership the organization began establishing branches in Gaesung, Incheon, Daegu, Busan, Jeonju, Gunsan, Hoeryung, Seongjin and Jeongpyung. The membership increased to 200 after two months of intensive effort. The income increased with more membership fees and could send more money to the interim government.

Christian women in Pyongyang formed an underground action group. Han Youngshin, a Presbyterian, invited female members of Presbyterian churches and organized this group. At this time, Methodist women also formed an underground action group on the suggestion of Park Seungil. These two groups had joint meetings several times and discussed detailed action plans. They decided to integrate following the suggestion of Kim Jeongmok and Kim Soonil who were officers of the interim government. They organized the Korea Patriotic Women's Group and established branches across the country. They raised independence funds from members and also from local female celebrities, and sent the funds to the interim government. They provided the interim government's officers with places to stay and connected them with other underground groups in Korea.

These activities of women were exceptional considering the social environment of Korea at that time. There were a few reasons that especially encouraged Christian women to participate in the March First Movement in an active way. First of all, women's groups were very well organized and active in churches and their experience in churches helped them organize and lead secret activities under Japan's oppression. In the case of Presbyterian churches, women's groups were first organized in 1898 and active in major cities in 1919. Methodist churches began organizing women's groups in 1897 and had women's groups in major cities in 1918. Secondly, most female intellectuals at that time were educated in Christian private schools. Graduates and students of Christian girls' schools were in close contact with one another and could play one of the central roles in the March First Movement. Thirdly, Japan's oppression of Christians also contributed to the active participation of Christian women in demonstrations. Women outnumbered men in churches at that time and churches strongly resisted Japan's oppression. Christian women's resistance to Japan was therefore much stronger than that of non-Christian women and they could participate in the March First Movement more actively than non-Christian women.

Christianity in Korea

After the independence

Education

Woman

Religion

Nation

Education

The Christian Academy
and the Christian Institute
for the Study of Justice and Development

The Christian Academy began as the Korea Christian Social Study Group, which was interested in building a culture of dialogue in Korean society. This group was organized by Rev. Kang Wonyong who had come back to Korea in 1959 after his study in the US. He was concerned about conservative pastors' support to President Rhee Syngman and even of his dictatorship because he was a Methodist elder. He was also concerned about the conflict between Christian fundamentalism and other religions. He thought that the education of people and the exchange of different religions could contribute to solve these social problems. This was the beginning of the Christian

Academy. At the beginning fifteen people participated in the study group. They would eat traditional rice soup together and discuss diverse social issues. A kind of group dialogue naturally began in Korea even before dialogue programs in other countries such as Germany's academy movement were introduced to Korea.

Rev. Kang Wonyong studied at Eunjin Middle School in Jiandao, China. He went to Japan and studied English literature in Meiji University. He engaged in education, rural and social activities in Jiandao and Manchuria, China and in Hoeryeong. After independence he studied at Korea Theological Seminary, the University of Manitoba in Canada and Union Theological Seminary in the US. He earned an honorary doctoral degree from the University of Manitoba in 1962. He was an educator in Seoul immediately after independence and held various posts in church organizations. In 1949 he succeeded Rev. Kim Jaejoon as the senior pastor of Kyungdong Church.

▶ Bupjung, Lee Moonyoung, Seo Namdong, Oh Jaeshik, Lee Geonhyo and Kang Wonyong gathered at the Christian Academy

The meeting between Kang Wonyong and Eberhard Müller provided a momentum for the Korea Christian Social Study Group to change to the Christian Academy. Müller was the founder of the academy movement in Germany. He heard about the activity of the Korea Christian Social Study Group and promised to support its activity. Kang Wonyong later recalled his dialogue with Müller as follows.

"I told him that social conditions in Korea are different from those of West Germany, other European countries and Japan. He emphasized that his support should be unconditional and Korea's academy movement must be Korean, responding to the Korean situation and led by Korean leaders."

The academy movement in West Germany began after the Second World War and had a great influence on German society. Müller was a prisoner of war and returned to Germany after the war. He found the country destroyed and the people frustrated and in crisis. He was in deep sorrow. He realized that the country had been psychologically ill even before the political failure and the war, and it lacked the spirit of dialogue and collaboration. He reached a conclusion that the country should have a campaign to provide people with spaces for dialogue and to encourage them to engage in dialogue. He wanted to revive in Germany the spirit of the ancient philosophers' dialogue and study of truth at the Akademia in Athens and called his campaign the academy movement. After getting Müller's promise of support Kang Wonyong called in about sixty members of the Korea Christian Social Study Group to the YMCA and asked about their opinions. Members agreed to accept the support. As a result, the Christian Academy officially began in May 1965 and the academy movement was launched.

One of the main activities that the Christian Academy engaged in after 1965 was the ecumenical movement among different churches and inter-faith dialogues. For example, the Christian Academy hosted a dialogue meeting bringing religious leaders of Protestant churches, Roman Catholic churches, Anglican churches and Buddhism together under the theme of 'common agendas of Korean religions.' Christian Academy would join Anglican churches' Easter worship services and send congratulatory cards to Buddhist temples on Buddha's birthday.

Kang Wonyong emphasized the education of progressive middle class people who were in between the conservative high class people and poor people. One effort he made was to teach female college students about feminism, which he had studied in the US. Some women who had studied with him later became NGO and political leaders.

Many progressive church leaders who were against Park Chunghee's Yushin government visited Kang Wonyong because he would sign on the statements urging Park Chunghee's resignation and democratization. Christian Academy became a cradle of the democratization movement.

In 1977, the Christian Academy's monthly magazine, *Dialogue* was discontinued because it had dealt with the stories of women workers oppressed by the government. In 1979, the Christian Academy experienced a crisis due to the so-called 'Christian Academy Incident.' Six staff including Lee Woojae who was in charge of rural affairs and Jeong Changryeol who was a professor of Hanyang University were arrested in March 1979. They were accused of reading banned books, promoting class consciousness and organizing an underground circle to build a socialist country. In the process of investigation, the Central Intelligence Agency illegally arrested their friends, people in relationship with the Christian Academy and its students. This agency tortured them and fabricated the incident, and meanwhile kept their families under house arrest. Nobody could visit them in prison. The Christian Academy and social leaders announced statements and sent petitions to the government. They revealed that the incident was fabricated and protested that the government was trying to damage the Christian Academy's activities on the excuse of anti-communism. The families of the defendants were continuously inspected and detained, and their human rights were severely violated. Petitioners were arrested by the agency. After one month of investigation, the incident that had been labeled as the exposure of a pro-communist circle was officially confirmed as a fabricated incident based on torture. The higher court found all defendants not guilty on the accusation of organizing a pro-communist circle. The Christian Academy changed its name to Korea Dialogue Academy at the 35th anniversary in May 2005 and

▶Defendants of the Christian Academy Incident and evidence presented in the case 天不變 外-巴 事件

reorganized some departments.

The Christian Institute for the Study of Justice and Development(CISJD) was founded on February 21, 1979 as a non-denominational organization. This organization integrated the Korea Christian Center for Industrial Study founded in December 1976 and the Korea Christian Academy of Sciences founded in January 1978. Rev. Kim Gwansuk founded the CISJD and Rev. Cho Seunghyuk was the first director and Dr. Kim Yongbok was the first vice director. The main purpose of CISJD was to contribute to building a just and democratic Korean society based on Christian spirit and ethics. It engaged in research on Christianity and industrialized Korean society, analyses of collected data, discussions, counseling for workers, reunification issues and publishing. The ultimate goal of all this work was to articulate and confirm the role of Christianity regarding the diverse problems of industrialized society. In 1982, CISJD carried out a survey on the 100th anniversary of Protestant churches in Korea and presented a new direction for Korean churches based on the collected data and analyzed statistics. It also carried out a separate survey to learn about non-Christians' understanding of churches and Christians, and the social status of churches. It published a report with the results of the survey including statistics and analyses. CISJD is supported by the Korean Methodist Church, the Presbyterian Church of Korea, the Presbyterian Church of the ROK and the National Council of Churches in Korea. It has cooperative relationships with the World Council of Churches, the Christian Council of Asia, the United Methodist Church and churches in Germany and the UK.

After
the independence

Woman

Women's Concerns about Gender Inequality
and National Divide

Korean Churches' Feminist Theology

Churches contributed to the modernization of
Korean society in the late Yi Dynasty. In particular, churches had
a great influence on the liberation of women who were oppressed
in the patriarchal Confucian society of Korea. The teachings of
the bible encouraged Koreans to respect men and women equally.
Women could naturally learn Hangul by reading the bible. Many
Christian schools provided women with educational opportunities
and contributed to the emergence of educated modernized
women. But the theology of Korean churches was based on
conservative ideas and supported the patriarchal Confucian
order. Churches individualized faith and oppressed women as

society did.

The theology based on conservative ideas greatly influenced the formation of women's faith in the early years of Korean churches. As a result, women considered Christ's salvation not as a real life event but as an afterlife matter. Women had a dichotomous understanding considering the human soul as important and body as insignificant. They projected God into their image of a father and understood the bible based on literal interpretations. They considered individual and social sufferings as realities that they must overcome with the grace of God.

Many unrecognized female mission workers made a huge contribution to the development and growth of Korean churches. In the early years of churches there were three kinds of women who were involved in social activities. First, there were women who overcame the obstacles of traditional Korean society and actively accepted the freedom the bible taught. They escaped from the oppression of patriarchal society and found their human characters. These women are Lee Kyungsook, Ha Lansa, Jeon Samdeok, Park Esther and Ju Lulu. Secondly, there were women who were very patriotic. These women had a strong will for independence and promoted their inner spirit of nationalism. Ryu Gwansoon, Kim Kyunghee, Kim Maria, Kang Giil and Chan Kyungshin were included in this category of women. Thirdly, some women were very actively engaged in promoting education, charity, missions and social work. These women were Bang Yein, Son Mere, Wang Jaedeok and Choi Naomi.

In the early years of Korean churches women had very active roles at individual and organizational levels. However, they were pushed to the periphery within churches with the gradual institutionalization of churches. The most prominent example of this change was the exclusion of women from ordination.

Feminist theology in the Korean churches began with the influence of Western feminist theologies. But feminist theology in Korea embraced these Western feminist theologies in a very critical way and struggled very much to develop an indigenous feminist theology. Feminist theology developed in the 1960s and 1970s in Western countries and was introduced to Korea in the 1980s. Women theologians in Korea struggled with basic women's issues in society and at the same time, national issues facing the divide of the Korean peninsula.

Many women's organizations were established based on feminist theology such as the Korea Church Women United, Korean Association of Women Theologians, Korea Academy of Feminist Theology, Christian Institute of Feminist Theology, Women's Church and Korea Association of Christian Women for Women Minjung.

The Korea Church Women United(KCWU) was

founded by church women from six denominations, the Korean Methodist Church, the Presbyterian Church of Korea, the Presbyterian Church of the ROK, the Lutheran Church in Korea, the Anglican Church of Korea and the Korean Evangelical Church in 1967. The foundation of this organization was a symbol of church women's solidarity. They articulated the purpose of the organization at the founding ceremony to work for churches' unity, respond to social agendas, develop women's leadership and build peace in the world. In 1975, the Year of Women was internationally announced and women's organizations around the world especially focused on women's awareness education. This trend of awareness education was introduced to Korea together with the new interpretation of the bible from the perspectives of feminist theology. Women theologians including Lee Woojeong who was then the president of the KCWU and Jang Sang who was a professor of Ewha Women's University, and some male theologians including Park Joonseo, a professor of Yonsei University, and Min Youngjin, a professor of the Methodist Seminary were engaged in the education of church women and guided them to feminist theology. They introduced women theologians like Letty Russell, Rosemary Ruether and Elizabeth Fiorenza and their works to Korea. Cho Hwasoon, Cho Youngsoon and Park Seongja, all ordained pastors, were especially engaged in the human rights movement. They integrated their field experiences into feminist theology and established the Korean Association of Women Theologians. The KCWU realized the urgent need for the alternative education of seminary graduates and held a seminar on the democratization of churches at the Academy House on January 22–23, 1979. This seminar was financially supported by the Asia Church Women United. Gong Deokgui, president of the KCWU, and Ahn Sangnim played the leading roles in organizing the seminar.

One of the most remarkable activities of the KCWU was its revelation of sex tourism in northeast Asian countries. They made the revelation in cooperation with Japanese women's church organizations. The problem of sex tourism caught international attention. It also shared the suffering of nuclear bombing victims with the public and urged the Japanese government to compensate the victims of war. It has been dealing with peace issues and especially engaged in anti-war and anti-nuclear campaigns.

The Korean Association of Women Theologians was founded on April 21, 1980. The founding ceremony was held at the Christian Building in Jongno 5-ga, Seoul and the KCWU assisted the foundation, taking responsibility for administrative matters. The Korean Association of Women Theologians articulated its goals to formalize and spread feminist theology in Korea, to contribute to church missions and to work for the establishment of a peaceful, just society.

Park Soonkyung was the first president of the association and suggested to define the term women theologians in terms of academic and at the same time, practical approaches. She presented a new definition saying "there is a need to redefine the term, theologians considering new trends of theologies. This term must include ordained pastors, program staff of church organizations, and even ordinary church women." The first officers of the association included Park Soongeum, Lim Choonbok, Lee Sooyoung, Lee Hyunsook, Lee Heesoo and Kim Hwaja. Choi Manja, Ahn Sangnim, Kim Yoonhee, Kang Youngja, Jang Sang, Na Seonjeong, Lee Moonwoo, Jang Seoksoon and Lee Yeonok also participated in the association as chairs of program committees and associate general secretaries.

The association held their first open seminar on July 14, 1980 at Saemoonan Church with the theme 'Women and Korean Churches.' This seminar was designed to recognize women's roles and enhance their status in the church. Their official bulletin was first published on April 17, 1981 and continued until the 12th volume. The bulletin then changed to the Korean Feminist Theology and the 75th volume was published recently. The association hosted the first conference of women theologians in 1983 with the support of the Ecumenical Association of Third World Theologians. It has been emphasizing solidarity with Asian women as well as Western women. It has been particularly focusing on the interpretation of the bible from women theologians' perspectives and the restoration of women's humanity, democratization of church communities, the national divide and reunification in the Korean peninsula and solidarity with Asian church women. The association is a non-denominational organization and spreading feminist theology to church women through distance learning programs and seminars.

The Korea Academy of Feminist Theology was founded by the agreement of the Korean Association of Women Theologians to take academic approaches to church women's issues. It had membership in the Korea Association of Christian Studies in 1985. The members of the organization have published the results of their collaborative studies such as *Experiences of Korean Women*(1994), *The Bible and Feminist Theology*(1995), *Churches and Feminist Theology*(1997), *Spirit and Feminist Theology*(1999), *Gender and Feminist Theology*(2001), *Multiculturalism and Feminist Theology*(2005) and *Media and Feminist Theology*(2012).

After
the independence

Religion

Contributions to Church Growth
and to the Dictatorship

The Evangelical Movement
of Korean Churches

24 Religion

Korean churches experienced remarkable growth between independence from the Japanese colonial rule and the mid-1990s. There were many reasons. After independence, the US military rule and the first government were friendly to churches. As a result of their church-friendly policies, society gradually became friendly to churches. The US was one of the superpowers leading the world and it was friendly to churches. Churches gave opportunities for many intellectuals to enter mainstream society.

The growth of churches was influenced by the

political and social instability of Korea. Churches provided people with religious comfort and spiritual shelter in the unstable environment caused by the Korean War and its aftereffects: poverty and political confusion. In the 1960s, the industrialization of the country began and many people moved to cities from the countryside. Churches were like a second hometown for them.

Mission campaigns played a very important role for churches' growth in Korea. After independence, Christians strongly felt that it was their responsibility to evangelize the entire nation and to make Korea the second Israel and the Korean people God's chosen people. They also thought that the evangelization of Korea was the key to solving many problems faced by Koreans. Evangelism was the most important value and the dominant historical trend in the Korean churches between independence and the 1980s.

In the 1950s, world-famous missionaries frequently visited Korea and led large-scale evangelical gatherings. The first government of President Rhee Syngman supported these Christian gatherings. At the time, Korean churches did not have technical skills and human resources to organize these big evangelical gatherings. Churches were not able to educate and empower Christians because they were experiencing an unprecedented divide involving theological controversies and conflicts over denominational authority that were building over the years. Churches were also in conflict about joining the WCC. Churches in fact needed to deal with these problems through internal communication within denominations but instead responded to the problems by immaturely taking sides.

In the 1960s, Korean churches experienced remarkable growth. After overcoming the crisis of the 1950s, churches could focus on internal matters and missions. The most prominent matter was the national evangelical movement in 1965. This movement contributed to uniting divided churches under the overarching cause of missions.

The national evangelical movement was led by Kim Whallan. On October 16, 1964, seventy five church leaders gathered at Ewha Women's University at the invitation of Kim Whallan. They discussed a comprehensive and active evangelical movement. They gathered several times more and finally chose a slogan for the movement, "Bringing Thirty Million to Christ." Almost all churches in Korea participated in this movement regardless of their inclination to progressive or conservative ideas.

In 1965, churches declared the 'Year of the National Evangelization' and launched a nationwide campaign. All denominations emphasized their own characteristics and strengths, and confirmed their efforts to save unbelievers. The essence of the national evangelization movement was public mission gatherings. The mission gatherings had two main subjects: anti-communism and evangelization. One of the famous figures who led successful gatherings was Rev. Cho Segwang, a Chinese missionary. He left his brothers in China and many Koreans were deeply touched by his own life stories that he shared in his sermons. In this year, more than a million people in total participated in mission gatherings. The number of Christians increased up to 10 percent of the total population.

In the 1970s and 1980s, the national evangelization movement reached its climax. The mega-size gatherings of the 1970s began with the mission gathering of Billy Graham in 1973. 'Explo 74' took place in 1974 and the 'Great Mission Gathering for National Evangelization' took place in 1977. These mega-size gatherings reached a climax with the 'Great Mission Gathering of World Evangelization' in 1980 and the 100th anniversary mission gathering in 1984.

When churches invited Rev. Billy Graham for the mega-size gathering, the central figure of this event was Rev. Han Kyungjik who had translated Billy Graham's sermons to previous mission gatherings in Korea. Yeouido Square in Seoul was used for mission gatherings after this event. Mission gatherings took place consecutively in local cities from May 16, 1973. Mega-size gatherings took place in Yeouido from May 30 to June 3 in 1973. Billy Graham only led Seoul gatherings. His sermons were simple with a message for people to invite Jesus Christ into their life and Rev. Kim Jeonghwan translated this message very well. George Beverly Shea accompanied Billy Graham and touched people's hearts with gospel songs. More than a million people participated in the last gathering. The Korean government shared the interest in issues of national security and anti-communism and actively supported these Christian gatherings.

In the next year, Explo 74 took place. People stayed and ate together in Yeouido Square for a week and participated in mission trainings. On the first day, 1.36 million people participated and the total number of participants for a week was 6.55 million. This was the highest number of participants in the history of mission gatherings. 300,000 officially registered in this event and participated in mission trainings. This event was led by Rev. Kim Joongon who was the representative of the Korea Campus Crusade for Christ(CCC). He had a dream of national evangelization as he prayed that God "let Korean young people dream of being followers of Jesus Christ, of saving all humans and of marching through global villages having the gospel in one hand and God's love in the other hand."

In 1977, the National Evangelization Gathering took place. This event was designed to commemorate the 70th anniversary of the Pyongyang Great Evangelization Gathering in 1907. In this event the Pyongyang gathering was acknowledged as the historical platform of the growth and evangelization of Korean churches. The subject of the gathering was 'for the national evangelization, by Koreans, with Holy Spirit.' The most important characteristic of this event was that Koreans played the central role in preparing for the event, raising funds and leading the event. This meant that Koreans began to organize and lead big mission gatherings that had usually been led by foreign missionaries. This event was led by Rev. Shin Hyungyun who had appeared on the stage in the 1960s and succeeded Rev. Lee Seongbong. He gradually became one of the main leaders of mission gatherings. Big gatherings for national evangelization continued in the 1980s.

The Korean churches grew rapidly during the national evangelization movement. The number of Christians increased to 12 million. Churches considered missions to be God's command and the most important character of their identity. Churches therefore devoted themselves to missions to follow God's command.

The national evangelical movement was also nationalistic. In the 1960s, churches presented Christians a new vision for Korea to become a Christian country and spiritually lead the world. This vision and God's calling became the new goal and pride of Koreans who were disappointed after the Japanese colonial rule and the national war. In the 1960s, Christianity was an alternative to help overcome spiritual panic and confusion.

Big mission gatherings had the explicit goal of evangelization. But in the 1970s, people suspected that the purpose of the gatherings was to calm down Christians' protests against the Yushin Constitution including the Namsan Easter

Common Worship and to encourage support of the Park Chunghee government. Explo 74 in August 1974 was the most typical event. This event was organized by Rev. Kim Joongon who was then the representative of CCC. He started a Presidential National Breakfast Prayer Meeting in 1966 and blessed the Yushin government in the 1973 meeting. He said "we have to make the Yushin government succeed with the blessing of God." He organized Explo 74 and made it successful with the active support of the Park Chunghee government. He and the CCC were strong supporters of the Yushin government.

In 1974, a series of political incidents such as Mincheonghakryun Incident and Inhyukdang Incident occurred under the fourth martial law. As a result, more than 1,000 people were arrested and 253 people were indicted. In this political environment, the evangelical movement was criticized for avoiding criticism of the situation and only focusing on the spread of the gospel, appealing emotionally to Christian youth and students, and encouraging distorted historical understanding. For example, William R. Bright said "there is no religious persecution in Korea. There is only political oppression and there is an obvious reason for that." He also argued "people were arrested because they had engaged in things they are not supposed to deal with. There is no country like Korea where people enjoy freedom to speak about Jesus Christ." This was a very inappropriate speech for an international Christian leader to officially make. The event that had invited him was very successful but it resulted in many Koreans' negative understanding of big mission gatherings.

Clear Meaning and Easy Reading

Publication of the Common Translation and the Standard New Translation of the Bible

25 Religion

In May 1957, a number of biblical scholars organized a committee for bible translation and decided to publish a newly translated bible. A few of the scholars called themselves 'friends of the bible' and translated 'The Gospel of Matthews' in 1961. This became the stepping stone of bible translation into modern language and inspired the Korean Bible Society.

The Roman Catholic Church had been reforming many areas since the second Vatican Council(1962–1965). One of the reforms was to translate the bible to indigenous languages so that priests and laypeople could easily understand the bible. As a result, Catholic churches around the world became engaged in bible translation. In addition, Protestant and Catholic churches were encouraged to translate the bible together. The United Bible Society(UBS) and the Bible Committee of the Vatican agreed to translate the bible together.

The Common Translation of the Old Testament and the New Testament was conducted in Korea. In January 1968, Protestant and Catholic churches organized a bible translation committee. On February 15 of the same year, the Old Testament translation committee was organized and Kim Jeongjoon, Jeong Yongseop, Bae Jaemin, Moon Ikwhan and Seon Jongwan began translation. Baek Mingwan, Huh Changdeok and Kim Changryeol from Catholic churches and Kim Jinman, Lee Geunseop and Park Changwhan from Protestant churches participated in the translation committee. The translation of the Old Testament and the New Testament was carried out simultaneously.

The participants in the translation committee agreed on two basic principles. First, they decided to follow the principles agreed on by the United Bible Society and the Vatican. Secondly, they agreed to use as original texts the Masoretic Text as published in Biblica Hebraica(the third edition edited by Rudolph Kittel in 1937) for the translation of the Old Testament, and the Greek New Testament(the first edition published in 1966 by the United Bible Society) for the translation of the New

Testament.

Regarding details, they agreed to avoid formal consistency in literal and formal translations and to focus on dynamic equivalent translations so that readers could clearly understand the contents and meanings of the original texts. They agreed to follow the proper names that Protestant and Catholic churches were using in their school textbooks and to use the pronunciations of the original language in case they could not find any use of proper nouns in Korean.

In April 1971, the New Testament was published after a long translation period. The Common Translation Bible with 1,997 pages of the Old Testament, 328 pages of the Apocrypha and 505 pages of the New Testament was finally published by the Korean Bible Society on Easter of 1977. The new edition of this bible was published in 1999, following new Korean spelling rules and correcting minor mistakes.

The Common Translation Bible had been used by a small number of Catholic, Orthodox and Anglican churches since its publication in 1977. Now only Anglican and Orthodox churches use it. The Korean Catholic Church published the Two Hundredth Anniversary New Testament to celebrate two hundred years of Korean missions in 1984 and chose the Catholic Bible as the official bible during Advent of 2005. The Common Translation Bible is now used in neither Catholic churches nor Protestant churches.

The Common Translation Bible was significant because Catholic and Protestant churches translated the bible together into contemporary Korean so that people could easily read and understand the teachings of the bible.

In the 1980s, there was a request from many ordained pastors and laypeople for a new translation of the bible. In response to this, the work on the Standard New Translation of the bible began. This work was not to correct or edit the previous translation but to translate the bible in a new way. The basic principle was to respect the spirit of the previous translation and the tradition of Korean churches. The translators of the Old Testament used the Hebrew Masoretic Text of the Biblica Hebraica Stuttgartensia(1967–1977) and the translators of the New Testament used the Greek New Testament(the third edition from 1983) as original texts.

The Standard New Translation Bible was published by the Korean Bible Society in January 1993. This was the result of ten years of work by sixteen theologians from different denominations. They used contemporary Korean for translation and this was the most important characteristic of this bible. They also used easy words so that everybody could understand the bible without difficulty. They worked very hard to deliver the meaning of the original text in a natural way. They wanted to deliver the contents and meanings of the Hebrew and Greek texts while also avoiding the unnatural styles of translated texts.

Another important characteristic of the Standard New Translation Bible was the new translation of the holy name of God, YHWH, which had been translated as 'Yeohowa(Jehovah)' for the previous translation and into 'Yahweh' for the Common Translation Bible. God was translated into 'Lord' in this work. The Masoretic Text of the Old Testament had the term 'Adonai' for the holy name of God and the Greek Text translated in the third century used the term 'Kyrios' for the holy name. The New Testament used 'Kyrios' and Jerome's Latin version(the *Vulgate*) had the term 'Dominus.' The German translation by Martin Luther used the term 'Herr' and many English versions of the bible used the term 'Lord' for the holy name. The translators of the Standard New Translation Bible followed these traditions of the Hebrew text, world churches and previous translations in Korea and they used the term meaning 'Lord' for the holy name of God, YHWH.

The characteristics of the Standard New Translation Bible can be summarized in four points. First, it avoided old fashioned words and used easy contemporary words. Secondly, it avoided the direct translation of Chinese characters into Korean and had natural Korean sentences. Thirdly, it was more Korean with correct grammar and full sentences and without meaningless phrases so that meanings could be delivered in a Korean way. Fourthly, it avoided sexually discriminatory expressions that could neglect women. For example, men used impolite, disrespectful language for women in the previous translation. But men and women verbally respected each other in this translation. It also avoided discriminatory expressions for the disabled.

Constant Alignment and Realignment of Churches

Divides on Denominational
and Theological Lines
and the Divide of Presbyterian Churches

26 Religion

The Presbyterian Church of Korea, which organized the first independent presbytery in 1907 and its general assembly in 1912, had maintained a single denomination. In the late years of the Japanese colonial rule, Presbyterian churches were assimilated into the Korea Presbyterian Church of Japan Christian Church(1943) and the Korea Christian Church of Japan Christian Church(1945). As a result, the identity of the Presbyterian Church was seriously damaged because the presbytery, the central decision making body was dissolved. The national independence from Japan in 1945 was a joyful event for Christians to rebuild the country and enjoy the freedom of faith again. Christians aimed to restore the identity of Korean churches and to reconstruct churches, but Presbyterian churches experienced several divisions in this period of reconstruction.

The first division of Presbyterian churches occurred in the Kyungnam Presbytery which covered the areas of Busan and Kyungsangnam-do. This presbytery was the center of the anti-Japan independence movement in the past. There were three groups in the presbytery when the country was freed from Japan and the presbytery was being reconstructed. The first group included a few pastors including Han Sangdong and Joo Namseon who had been arrested for their refusal to worship at Japanese shrines. They were freed upon the independence of the country. The second group was led by the pastors including Kim Changdong who had actively supported Japan. The last group included most people who had chosen not to resist Japan.

The freed pastors and laypeople were active in reconstructing the presbytery. In the 47th Assembly of the presbytery, Rev. Joo Namseon was assigned to be moderator and the correction of past wrong doings emerged as the most important agenda item. Rev. Han Sangdong planned to establish a new theological seminary under the supervision of the presbytery in cooperation with Rev. Park Yoonseon and Rev. Joo Namseon. There was already a theological seminary at that time. But this seminary had worshipped at Japanese shrines and supported a more progressive trend of theology. Many pastors who supported conservative theological trends disliked this seminary. Under these circumstances Han Sangdong planned to establish a new seminary to take the place of the Pyongyang Theological Seminary that had been closed due to its resistance to worshipping at Japanese shrines. On September 20, 1946, the Korea Seminary opened in Busanjin. This seminary rented a classroom from a local school and Park Yoonseon was assigned to be the first dean. As a result, the Kyungnam Presytery and the Korea Seminary became focal points for the pastors who had resisted Japan and had been released from prison.

In the 48th Assembly in December 1946, Rev. Kim Gilchang who had actively supported Japan was elected as the moderator. This changed the whole situation. Kim Gilchang criticized the Korea Seminary, cancelled the permission to run the seminary, and banned pastors' recommendations of students. Han Sangdong strongly resisted these abrupt decisions and withdrew from the presbytery. Many churches supported Han Sangdong and resisted the decisions. They released a statement supporting Han Sangdong. The presbytery had a special meeting in March 1947 and dismissed Kim Gilchang and other officers. This meeting decided to reconstruct the presbytery with the pastors who had resisted Japan and been released from prison. Han Sangdong cancelled his withdrawal and returned to the presbytery. The Korean Seminary regained the presbytery's permission and the relationship between the presbytery and the seminary was restored.

But the problem began with an unexpected

event. In the 50ᵗʰ Assembly(December 1948), one person stood up and repented his worship at Japanese shrines in the late years of Japanese colonial rule. Then Han Sangdong suggested dismissing Kim Gilchang from the status of ordained pastor. Kim Gilchang faced the crisis of being dismissed. He organized his supporters and established a separate presbytery together with them. As a result, the Kyungnam presbytery was divided into two and sent different representatives to the 35ᵗʰ General Assembly(April 1949) of the Presbyterian Church. The General Assembly acknowledged the representative status of the Kyungnam presbytery and demanded it to cut its relationship with missionaries including Bruce F. Hunt who had left the US Northern Presbyterian Church. The General Assembly tried to solve the problem of the separation and made a special committee which suggested dividing the Kyungnam presbytery into three rather than integrating it by force. Then the Kyungnam presbytery with the leadership of the previously arrested pastors considered that the General Assembly was supporting the separate presbytery led by Kim Gilchang. The presbytery leaders strongly criticized the General Assembly's decision to divide the presbytery into three. They decided to rename the Kyungnam Presbytery, the Kyungnam Legal Presbytery. The General Assembly and the Kyungnam Legal Presbytery fiercely confronted each other from this time onward.

The 36ᵗʰ General Assembly, which had been suspended due to the Korean War and resumed in 1951, did not recognize the delegates of the Kyungnam Legal Presbytery. They then organized an independent general assembly at Sungnam Church in Jinju in 1952. This was the beginning of the Goshin branch of the Presbyterian Church. This separation was the result of Presbyterian churches' inability in the past to solve the problem of worshipping at Japanese shrines.

In the next year, the leaders of the General Assembly agreed to reintegrate the separated denominations and suggested two main things to the Goshin branch. First, the General Assembly could repent of the sin of worshipping at Japanese shrines in the past, although it had decided to stop the worship at Japanese shrines in 1946. Secondly, it could integrate the Korea Seminary into the Presbyterian Theological Seminary and assign Rev. Park Hyungryong as the vice dean. It could also recognize the pastors who had graduated from the Korea Seminary as pastors of the Presbyterian Church. In response to these suggestions the Goshin branch asked the General Assembly to make a statement acknowledging its mistake to cut off the graduates of the Korea Seminary.

In the 39th General Assembly in 1954, Rev. Lee Wonyoung was elected as the moderator. He had resisted Japanese shrines and was arrested in the past. He was recognized as a faithful pastor and respected by people. Most delegates to the General Assembly considered that the root cause of the separation was the past problem of worshipping at Japanese shrines and therefore, that the General Assembly first had to repent the sin. The General Assembly recognized this idea and announced a statement saying "we recognize that the decision of the 27ᵗʰ General Assembly to worship at Japanese shrines was a sin before God and we repeal the decision." But the reintegration of the Goshin branch was not accomplished.

The Presbyterian Church was approaching to another divide in the last days of the Korean War. The root of the problem was the Chosun Seminary. This seminary was begun by Kim Jaejoon, Song Changgeun and Chae Pilgeun. They wanted to establish a new theological seminary to educate future pastors after the Pyongyang Theological Seminary had voluntarily closed due to the problem of worshipping at Japanese shrines. The Chosun Seminary began in 1940 with the permission of the General Assembly.

After independence the 32ⁿᵈ General Assembly in 1946 permitted the direct management of the Chosun Seminary because it was then the only seminary of the Presbyterian Church. But some people who criticized Rev. Kim Jaejoon's theological understanding constantly complained about the curriculum of the seminary. In this situation some conservative students opposed Kim Jaejoon. Fifty one students who criticized Kim Jaejoon's faith and biblical understanding sent a petition to the General Assembly. The General Assembly made an eight-member committee to investigate the matter. Kim Jaejoon and his colleague, Song Changgeun were called for investigation. Kim Jaejoon presented the General Assembly with a written statement that articulated his biblical understanding and theological position. The investigation committee could not easily refute Kim Jaejoon's argument of 'conservative faith, progressive theology.' But Park Hyungryong continued criticizing Kim Jaejoon's theological position even during the investigation.

At this time, the establishment of a new theological seminary was being discussed in Seoul. A Presbyterian Theological Seminary was finally established with the support of US missionaries and the assignment of Park Hyungryong as the dean. In June 1948, this new seminary officially opened and was recognized as a Presbyterian seminary in the 35th General Assembly in 1949. As a result, the Presbyterian Church had two seminaries. The 36th General Assembly in 1951 repealed the status of the Chosun Seminary as the Presbyterian seminary in spite of its strong resistance. The problem began here.

The 37th General Assembly decided to dismiss Kim Jaejoon and to send William Scott back to his country, Canada. It also decided not to recruit the graduates of the Chosun Seminary. The Gyeonggi Presbytery that Kim Jaejoon was affiliated with strongly resisted the decision but the 38th General Assembly in 1953 reconfirmed the dismissal of Kim Jaejoon. The situation was becoming irrevocable and people supporting the Chosun Seminary and Kim Jaejoon had a separate 38th General Assembly at the Chosun Seminary in June. They called it the Legal General Assembly and founded a new denomination with the ideas of 'freedom of the gospel and faith, spirit of independence and self-support, and spirit of the world church.' The mission department of the Presbyterian Church of Canada that had maintained a good relationship with the Chosun Seminary supported this new denomination. In the next year, the name of denomination was changed to the Presbyterian Church in the Republic of Korea(PROK). The Presbyterian churches divided again due to different theological positions.

Most Presbyterian churches remained in the Presbyterian Church of Korea(PCK) even after the separation of the Goshin branch and the PROK. But the PCK experienced its biggest separation before long. The PCK's application to membership in the WCC, Park Hyungryong's resignation relating to the seminary site and delegates of the Gyeonggi Presbytery had a big influence on the separation.

In 1948, the foundation assembly of the WCC took place in Amsterdam. Rev. Kim Gwansuk participated in the assembly. He suggested the PCK to join the WCC and the General Assembly accepted the suggestion. But conservative members of the PCK were critical about the WCC. Twenty two Christian congressmen announced a statement during the Korean War and criticized the WCC for recognizing communism. As a result, more conservative pastors opposed the WCC. In the meantime, the National Association of Evangelicals(NAE) was founded in the US and the World Evangelical Fellowship(WEF) was founded by conservative organizations in the world to confront the WCC in 1951. In Korea, conservative pastors including Park Hyungryong and Jeong Gyuho established the Korean Association of Evangelicals and joined the WEF in 1955. They built an international working relationship with the WEF and led a campaign resisting the PCK's participation in the WCC.

The 41st General Assembly had to deal with the issue of participation in the WCC and decided to organize an ecumenical study committee that could carry out research and report its results at the General Assembly. There was already a clear divide within the PCK between proponents and opponents of the WCC. The committee was organized with four opponents including Park Hyungryong and four proponents including Han Kyungjik. The committee worked for a year and presented a report to the 42nd General Assembly in 1957. But the report did not have any conclusion and only suggested that the PCK could oppose the ecumenical movement of the WCC and only participate in the fellowship and cooperation work of the WCC in a selective way.

At this time, an incident occurred and made the conflict between the opponents and proponents more complicated. In 1953 after the Armistice Agreement of the Korean War, the PCK tried to move its seminary to a historical site in Namsan and gain the government's permission for the site. Then Park Hyungryong who was leading the opposition group and the dean of the seminary lost 30 million won to a swindler in the process of acquiring the site. He decided to take responsibility for the incident and resigned. In March 1958, the board meeting of the seminary accepted his resignation. But the opponents of the WCC supported him and resisted the board decision. They even argued that Park Hyungryong's resignation would result in the retreat of conservative theology and the growth of progressive, communist theology.

A scandal relating to the Gyeonggi Presbytery delegates had a more direct influence on the division of the PCK. The 72nd Assembly of the Gyeonggi Presbytery(May 1959) was supposed to elect its delegates to the General Assembly. At this time, the opponents and proponents of the WCC were in an intense competition with each other to have more delegates to send to the General Assembly. The Gyeonggi Presbytery was controlled by the proponents. It was therefore expected that the proponent side would have more delegates. The result unexpectedly showed the overwhelming victory of the opponent side. But this was because of a mistake in the ballot counting. The proponent side had an extraordinary assembly in June and overwhelmingly won the election.

The 44th General Assembly in 1959 had national attention. The two sides of the Gyeonggi Presbytery presented different lists of delegates. The General Assembly decided to take a vote to choose one list. The delegates of the proponent side gained more votes and could attend the General Assembly. But the opponent side did not accept the result and raised a question about the representation of the proponent delegates. Then the moderator Rev. Noh Jinhyeon who opposed the WCC had a separate meeting with other officers and former moderators, and proposed a solution that reversed the previous decision. His proposition was to suspend the General Assembly until November 24, two months later, and to ask the Gyeonggi Presbytery to solve the problem. He did not explicitly ask pros and cons, and the proposition passed. Rev. Ahn Gwangkook then jumped up to the podium and announced a proposition of non-confidence in the officers and passed it. The proponent side resumed the General Assembly in Yeondong Church in the next day. The opponent side waited until November 24 as Rev. Noh Jinhyeon had declared and resumed the General Assembly in Seongdong Church. Two Presbyterian groups with similar power formed separate general assemblies.

One month later a committee for integration was organized. The committee proposed integration measures to both sides. The proposal had three major points: "1. The PCK

▶ Extraordinary Geyeonggi Presbytery Assembly in June 29, 1959 at Seongdong Church

maintains the seventy five years of faith tradition; 2. The PCK withdraws from the WCC and the ICCC(NAE) for the peace and unity of the General Assembly; 3. The two sides discuss mission policies and carry them out together." The officers of the Presbyterian Church of USA visited Korea on November 9 and first met the integration committee and the two sides separately. They also hosted a joint meeting together with the Presbyterian Church of Australia inviting the two sides. The two sides had eight meetings until January 1960 together with the representatives from the US and Australian Presbyterian churches. They tried to find a way to reintegrate the PCK. But on January 15, the effort for integration ended without any positive results.

On February 13, 1960, the opponent side formed the Presbyterian Church Hapdong together with the Goshin branch. But this new denomination was divided again into the Goshin and Hapdong on November 19, 1962. However, some delegates from the two sides, delegates with neutral positions and the representatives of the US and Australian churches gathered at Saemoonan Church on February 17, 1960, a few days after the formation of the PC Hapdong, and held the PCK General Assembly(Tonghap). They still wanted the unity of the PCK. The effort for the reintegration of the PCK Tonghap and the PCK Hapdong was made but the unity of Presbyterian churches was not accomplished.

Divide of Methodist churches

The Korean Methodist Church(KMC) experienced three times of division after the independence of the country. The Korea Christian Church of the Japan Christian Church was founded in the late years of the Japanese colonial rule. After independence the officers of this denomination changed its name to the Korea Christian Church and had a meeting on September 8, 1945. The purpose of this meeting was to maintain the structure of the Korea Christian Church. This church was very cooperative with Japan in the past and most participants in the meeting were church leaders who had been active in cooperating with Japan. They wanted to make an integrated denomination and maintain their control over the church.

Dozens of participants including Rev. Lee Gyugap were enraged and left the meeting. They did not recognize the Korea Christian Church and wanted to reconstruct the Methodist denomination. They organized a committee to rebuild the Methodist church and held a district meeting at Dongdaemoon Church in January 1946. They also began a theological education program. This group that was called 'Jaegeonpa(Reconstruction Group)' refused all the structures and rules that had been made after the inauguration of Bishop Jeong Choonsu who was known as one of the prominent pro-Japan figures. Participants in the Jaegeonpa had been excluded by pro-Japan church leaders for a long time. Other denominations such as the Presbyterian Church and the Baptist Church were also discussing reconstructing independent churches at this time. In this situation the Korea Christian Church was dissolved before long. The pro-Japan Methodist leaders who wanted to maintain the Korea Christian Church and at the same time their privilege faced a difficult situation.

The active participants in the Korea Christian Church gathered at Soopyokyo Church in September 1946 and held a meeting to restore the Korea Christian Church. This group that was called 'Bokheungpa(restoration group)' confronted with the Jaegeonpa. The two groups criticized each other and competed to gain the support of individual churches. The Jaegeonpa did not have much support within the Methodist church but gradually strengthened its influence with the participation of pastors from the area that is now North Korea. The two groups separately had district meetings and general conferences and elected bishops. The Methodist church was eventually divided into two. But the divide did not last long. A joint general conference took place on April 29, 1949, four years after the divide. This conference was the result of the unity campaign led by some lay youth leaders including Moon Changmo, Park Hyunsook and Jang Sewhan.

In 1953, the Methodist Church had to elect a new bishop as the term of Bishop Ryu Hyunggi was about to end. Most people supported renewing his term because the church desperately needed the financial support of US Methodist churches for the restoration of churches after the Korean War and Ryu Hyunggi was very close to the US churches. The problem was the constitution that regulated two year terms for the position of bishop. The supporters of Ryu Hyunggi presented an amendment to extend the term to four years but others opposed the amendment. In this situation, the general conference was postponed to the next year. In the meantime, there was a scandal relating to an investment mistake and a big loss of mission funds. But Ryu Hyunggi was reelected as bishop with the overwhelming support of delegates. His opponents were enraged and left the room. They organized the Hoheonpa(Constitution Protection Group) and insisted on non-confidence in the bishop. The Chongriwon that supported Ryu Hyunggi strongly reacted to the Hoheonpa by suspending or dismissing the church positions of the participants in the group. This conflict was a reiteration of the confrontation between the Jaegeonpa and Bokheungpa. The participants in the Chongriwon had participated in the Jaegeonpa and the participants in the Hoheonpa in the Bokheungpa in the past. On the other hand, a regional conflict between the West District in the North and the Central District in the South influenced the denominational conflict. The Hoheonpa eventually held a national meeting at Cheonan Jeil Church in March 1954 and elected Rev. Kim Uengtae as bishop. The Methodist Church was divided again into the Hoheon Conference and the Chonriwon. But the financial and human foundation of the Hoheon Conference was very weak and Ryu Hyunggi's term ended. The two groups had a joint meeting in 1959 and elected Rev. Kim Jongpil as bishop. They united again.

The Methodist Church was divided again in the 1970s. The Hoheonpa competed with the Sungwhapa from the West District in the North to control the denomination. The conflict escalated and people who were concerned about the conflict formed 'Chungdongpa.' The Methodist Church was in chaos due to these three groups' confrontations. In 1970, a group that complained about the result of the Central District's bishop election left the district and formed an independent district, Gyeonggi District at Incheon Soongui Church in March 1971. This district held a general conference in 1975 and founded an independent denomination.

The KMC experienced a conflict again in 1974 relating to the election of a bishop in the 12th General Conference. The main parties of this conflict were the Hoheonpa and the group that had belonged to the West District in the past. A pastor of the Hoheonpa was elected as bishop and some delegates left the room. They formed a separate denomination called the Korean Methodist Church Gaengsin(renewal) and had a separate general conference at Jonggyo Church. Some churches and foreign missionaries expressed neutral positions concerning the divide of the denomination. Now the Methodist Church was divided into four groups, the Chongriwon(former Hoheonpa), the Gaengsin General Conference that was against the Chongriwon, the United General Conference and the neutral group. The Chongriwon was opposed by the other three groups that announced a statement of unity in November 1975 and held a joint general conference. In 1978, the Chonriwon and the united general conference were reintegrated. The Methodist Church became one church again.

The KMC suffered from divides after the independence of the country like the PCK did. The three times of divide were rooted in the regional conflict and power struggles within the denomination. There was no conflict over theological positions and the KMC could be finally united again after three periods of divide.

Christian Heresies

"We reject Shincheonji(meaning a new world) followers."

This kind of message is easily found in front of many churches in Korea now. This shows how much Shincheonji disturbs Korean churches. On September 3, 2012, the head of Tongilgyo(Unification Church) Moon Sunmyung died at the age of ninety two and Tongilgyo captured the media attention. Many people are now curious about who will succeed his leadership. God's Church is one of the most active heresies in Korea. These three, Shincheonji, Tongilgyo and God's Church are major Christian heresies in Korea now.

Churches grew rapidly in Korea after the country's independence from the Japanese colonial rule in 1945. The US military administration immediately after the independence provided churches with favorable conditions for growth. The Korean War killed about three million people and made Koreans think about the afterlife. In the 1960s, with the country's industrialization many people moved to cities from the countryside. Churches in cities became alternative communities for these newcomers that bound them together and provided them with comfort. At this time, churches, for their part, devoted their energies to the evangelization of the nation. Most church leaders dreamed of building a Christian country.

Many new Christian sects joined the energetic religious field at this time. These sects had a peculiar tendency to deify their founders who purported to have mysterious experiences and God's calling. This clearly showed Korean heresies' mysticism. The bible was abused to deify their founders. They did not translate the bible contextually but misused the teachings and stories of the bible to justify the founders' individual experiences and callings. The bible was fully distorted.

The heresy founders' argument of mysterious experiences damaged Christian monotheism and challenged the legitimacy of Christianity. They argued that Christ's salvation had been fulfilled by them. Most heresies insisted on a particular eschatology and forced their followers to believe the founders' teachings without raising any questions. The followers dreamed of a new paradise on earth and a heaven that would be built by their initiatives. Religious blessings were the essential element of the heresies and at the same time, the foundation of their development. They usually began with individual mysterious experiences and callings, challenged the bible and Christianity itself, and finally gave people distorted ideas about the end times.

The most prominent heresies that emerged after independence were Tongilgyo, Jeondogwan and Dongbanggyo. In the 1960s, Eden Christian Monastery, Dongbanggyo, Seil Church and Isaac Church taught about eschatology and rapidly grew. In the late 1970s, Jeong Myungseok's Aecheon Church taught about eschatology and God's Church was prepared for the Second Advent at Jeonyui Mountain in Yeongi-gun, Chungcheongnam-do in 1988. The distorted eschatology reached the climax when Lee Janglim's Dami Mission insisted that the rapture would be on October 28, 1992. Churches have not been dealing with eschatology theologically because of the aftereffect of the heresies' distorted eschatology.

The most problematic heresies now in Korea are Tongilgyo, Shincheonji and God's Church. Tongilgyo was founded by Moon Sunmyung in 1954. He systematized a theory that regarded sexual depravation as the origin of sin. The sin of Adam and Eve was also understood as connected to a sexual crime. This is one peculiar characteristic of Korean heresies that originated from Kim Seongdo who had called himself 'New Lord' in the 1920s. His interpretation of the bible was not based on serious studies of the bible but came out of private religious experience. His argument about lewdness and the Second Advent was transferred to Moon Sunmyung through Kim Baekmoon who had been one of followers of Kim Seongdo. In this context, Kim Seongdo can be regarded as the founder of all Christian heresies in Korea. Tongilgyo argues that Jesus Christ did not accomplish salvation and that Moon Sunmyung will accomplish the duty. This is the most problematic part of Tongilgyo.

Tongilgyo adopted anti-communism and was protected by the US and the Korean military government in the 1960s and 1970s. It then engaged in the arms industry and gained enormous profit. Tongilgyo built a close relationship with the Park Chunghee government, supporting the government's anti-communism policies. New religions usually take a pro-government position to gain the attention and acknowledgment of the government and society. They support politicians in order to build religious facilities and gain permissions from public agencies. Politicians build working relationships with new religions to get donations and votes. Tongilgyo manipulated this kind of symbiotic relationship in an efficient way. Tongilgyo moved its focus from anti-communism to reunification in the late 1980s. Moon Sunmyung met Mikhail Gorbachev in Russia and Kim Il Sung in North Korea.

Moon Sunmyung was at the center of many controversies until he passed away in 2012. But Tongilgyo is very different from other small sects and it maintained its religious foundation. Its doctrines have been systematized, and its churches are well organized. Tongilgyo has established a very stable structure based on its relations with the economic sector in Korea and the world. Tongilgyo is not just a sect but has already become an institutionalized religion. But the conflict between Tongilgyo and Christian churches will continue as long as Tongilgyo refuses to give up its identity based on Christianity.

Shincheonji is the most problematic heresy in Korea now. It was founded by Lee Manhee in 1984. He insisted that he was the revelation of Holy Spirit. He was influenced by Park Taeseon, the founder of Jeondogwan and Yoo Jaeyeol, the founder of Jangmak-Sungjoen. Park Taeseon was a famous preacher who attracted hundreds of thousands of people to his gatherings. He built a religious community called Shinangchon in the 1960s and 1970s. In this period Joendogwan surpassed Tongilgyo in terms of the number of followers and its power. Jangmak-Sungjeon, founded by Yoo Jaeyeol in 1966, declared that judgment day would be on November 1, 1969. Many believers gathered at Cheonggye Mountain in Seoul which they regarded as the shelter in the judgment day. He intensively read the books of Daniel, Ezekiel, and Zechariah in the Old Testament and Revelation in the New Testament, and preached about signs of the judgment day and salvation. Many followers of Jeondogwan agreed with him and joined Jangmak-Sungjoen. Lee Manhee also joined this sect and later founded Shincheonji.

Shincheonji followers have been focusing on missions, arguing that they can be kings and priests when the number of believers reaches 144,000. Churches have experienced difficulties for a long time due to their missions. They also have a very negative influence on Korean society as a whole. They disturb churches and lure Christians to their churches using senseless ways of missions. It is said that the most effective way to avoid Shincheonji is not to participate in bible studies outside churches.

God's Church, founded in 1964, has experienced more stable growth than other new religious sects. It is rooted in the Seventh Day Adventist Church. It believes in Ahn Sanghong as the reincarnation of Christ and God, and Jang Gilja as the mother of the New Jerusalem and God the Mother. It argues that there is also God the Mother and emphasizes the Passover in the Old Testament in relation to salvation. These are the most peculiar things of God's Church. Like Tongilgyo, it is actively engaged in overseas missions. This shows the internationalization of new religious sects in Korea. God's Church tries to make a good social image participating in social matters. But its arguments are far from Christian teachings. The continuous emergence and growth of new religious sects in Korea based on Christianity challenge churches to engage in theological and logical studies of Christianity in an organized way. Churches must learn lessons from these heresies that constantly challenge

Christian faith and from the society that enables their emergence and growth.

Support to Dictatorship
and Constitutional Amendment

Conservative Churches
and the Birth of the Christian Council
of Korea

28 Religion

> *"I reached a conclusion after talking to many people around me that the culture of the Christian Council of Korea(CCK) cannot be changed. The CCK must be eliminated. Its reform is not possible. There is no need for a substitution."*

Son Bongho, a professor of the Goshin Seminary made this answer to a question in a report in February 2011.

Churches objectively reflected on the role of churches after the April 19 Revolution and carefully sought a positive role for churches in society. In 1964, the country faced the crisis of the Korea–Japan summit and churches began speaking about political matters and dealing with social issues.

Churches' participation in society in the 1960s is largely divided into two stages. One was the churches' campaign against the unjust Korea–Japan summit and the normalization of diplomatic relations with Japan in 1964. The other was churches' protest against the Korea–Japan Agreement in June 1965. But not all churches joined the protest. Most pastors in fact were silent and some church leaders even criticized churches' participation in politics. The churches' protest was irreversible in spite of this criticism and most churches were of one voice opposing the Korea–Japan Agreement. Through this protest, churches could be reborn as the watchdog of military dictatorship with a prophetic voice and also as a champion of human rights and democratization.

In 1969, the Park Chunghee government tried to amend the constitution to allow him a third term. This political trick stimulated churches to consider their political position seriously. Progressive church leaders including Yoon Boseon, Ham Seokheon, Kim Jaejoon, Lee Byunglin, Jang Joonha and Kim Gwansuk opposed the amendment and announced their position together with two opposition leaders, Kim Daejung and Kim Youngsam.* By contrast, conservative church leaders

* These two persons later served as the fourteenth and fifteenth presidents.

including Han Kyungjik, Park Hungryong, Cho Yonggi, Kim Joongon, Kim Jangwhan and Kim Yoonchan organized the Christian Association of Korea with 242 pastors and announced their support to the amendment in a statement saying "we want strong leadership in Korea." As a result, churches were divided into two major groups, the progressive side which supported the NCCK and the conservative side which supported the Christian Association of Korea.

The leaders from pro-government conservative churches built a close relationship with high ranking officers of the military government. They maintained a cooperative relationship between their churches and the government in a systemic way. The Presidential National Prayer Breakfast, begun on May 1, 1968, was one of the most prominent cases of this close relationship and cooperation.

Kim Joongon who had played the central role in starting the Presidential National Prayer Breakfast Meeting founded the Korea Campus Crusade for Christ(Korea CCC). The growth of the CCC showed the symbiotic relationship between churches and the government. The government granted part of the former Russian Embassy site to the CCC despite Seoul City's protest. In response to the government's full support, the CCC was actively engaged in campus missions to mislead college students' interest in political issues to anti-communism and to prevent their participation in protests such as April 19 Revolution.

With big support from the government, conservative churches hosted mega-size mission gatherings such as the National Evangelization Movement, Anti-communism and National Security Gathering, Billy Graham Mission Gathering and Explo 74. These events contributed to the rapid growth of conservative churches. The close relationship between the government and conservative churches continued even after the Gwangju Massacre in May 1980. On August 6, 1980 when the country was still in confusion after the Gwangju Massacre, they hosted the so-called Prayer Breakfast Meeting for the Country to give a blessing to the illegitimate new government. This meeting was aired publically and the real face of conservative churches was also revealed to the entire country.

In the prayer meeting, Rev. Han Kyungjik and Rev. Chung Jinkyung led prayers for Chun Doohwan who had ordered the Gwangju Massacre and then was the chair of National Security Committee. Han Kyungjik prayed "God, let him have courage like Joshua had in the bible" and Chung Jinkyung legitimized his control praying "he was sent by God to take the important position and eliminate the sins of society in this difficult situation."

In 1989, these conservative church leaders including Han Kyungjik founded the Christian Council of Korea(CCK) to focus on evangelization and to criticize the human rights and democratization movements of the NCCK. Other conservative church leaders and some conservative pastors who were in cooperation with the NCCK also joined the CCK. This became the biggest conservative church organization in Korea.

In the statement announced at the founding Assembly on December 28, 1989, the CCK articulated "we wish all protestant churches and church organizations and leaders to participate in the CCK. We wish to unite and cooperate with one another to fulfill the authentic duty of churches." The statement argued that the CCK was founded to overcome the divides of Korean churches and unite them all.

The CCK has engaged in humanitarian campaigns such as the rice sending campaign for North Korea,

▶ Founding Assembly Worship of the CCK

the refugee protection campaign and support to North Korean refugees. These social campaigns of the CCK are not fundamentally contrasting to the NCCK's participation in social issues now, because the democratic government came to power in the 1990s, and the NCCK's position is less progressive compared to the 1970s and 1980s due to the new membership of conservative denominations.

The history of the NCCK's participation in social issues is long. In particular, the NCCK's protest against the dictatorship in the 1970s and 1980s was famous inside and outside churches. The CCK could not compete with the NCCK in terms of expressing concerns about political issues. It would only announce statements when the NCCK strongly criticized the government. Lee Manyeol, who is an honorary professor of Sookmyung Women's University and the former chair of National Institute of Korean History, points out that the CCK is the association of conservative churches and its root is the Christian Association of Korea that supported the constitutional amendment for Park Chunghee's third term.

In January 2011, the CCK was caught in a big scandal because of the press conference of the former moderator Lee Gwangseon. He was involved in the CCK's money politics and corrupt election. There have been strong voices asking for the disintegration of the CCK since then. Sixteen Christian groups organized a network to disintegrate the CCK. On July 26, 2011, 100 Christian lay leaders from conservative and progressive sides announced a statement urging the disintegration of the CCK.

But the CCK did not care about the criticism and tried to settle the scandal by accepting the 'July 7 Reform Statute' that had been suggested in an extraordinary assembly on July 7, 2011. But this trial was even failed when the standing committee nullified the July 7 Reform Statute. As a result, the members from the PCK, Goshin, Baeksuk, Daeshin, Full Gospel Church and Holiness Church began confronting the CCK's leadership.

As of October 2012, the members from the PCK, Baekseuk, Hanyoung and Hansin have withdrawn from the CCK and the Daeshin, Gisung, Nasung, Yesung and Baptist Church stated reservations. The CCK has become an association of members from the PC Hapdong and small denominations. Thirty denominations and nine organizations that withdrew from the CCK have founded the Korean Association of Churches.

Nation

New Covenant between Flood and Rainbow
JPIC Convocation

29 Nation

Dietrich Bonheoffer argued the need for a universal Christian peace council at an ecumenical assembly in 1934. In 1982, the World Association of Reformed Churches(WARC) urged making a covenant for peace and justice. In 1983, the participants of the WCC 6th Assembly in Vancouver agreed that the covenant for justice, peace and the integrity of creation was the churches' historical responsibility and this must be a priority of the WCC programs. Dietrich Bonheoffer's argument in 1934 was eventually revived for realization.

The WCC 5th Assembly in Nairobi presented the

agenda for a just, participatory and sustainable society(JPSS) that churches in the world must struggle with together. This was the sign of changing directions in churches' participation in social issues. After the Nairobi Assembly, the JPSS campaign became one of the major agendas for churches that were deeply concerned about structural problems in societies and natural destruction. This campaign was connected to the WCC 6th Assembly in Vancouver and the justice, peace and the integrity of creation(JPIC) campaign. Churches courageously faced the comprehensive contradictions of the world caused by political and economic inequality, structural problems, environmental destruction, nuclear arms and the gradual depletion of food and resources. Churches seriously questioned the sustainability of human community. Only in 1987 did the UN include the term sustainable development in one of its reports. The churches' initiative of raising questions about sustainability was therefore much earlier than that of other institutions in the world. In 1992, the UN Conference on Environment and Development took place in Rio de Janeiro, Brazil and the international community agreed to deal with environmental issues jointly. In this context, the meaning and status of the WCC's JPIC Convocation held in Seoul in 1990(earlier than the UN effort) must be newly evaluated.

In 1988, the WCC Central Committee decided to hold the JPIC Convocation on March 5-13, 1990 in Seoul. The Korean churches' hosting of the JIPC Convocation had two meanings. On the one hand, the WCC recognized the Korean churches' history of sacrifice for and devotion to justice and peace. Seoul had a historical significance and therefore was an appropriate place to discuss justice, peace and the integrity of creation. On the other hand, Seoul was a place suffering from rapid industrialization, from the widening gap between the haves and have-nots and from environmental destruction. Seoul was facing all the problems the JIPC Convocation was supposed to deal with.

On March 5, 1990, the JPIC Convocation began with more than 1,000 participants from around the world. The WCC described the need for this convocation in the statement that people were living between the Flood and the Rainbow. People's lives were being threatened. but at the same time people were living in God's covenant for a new heaven and a new earth.

► The opening worship of the JPIC Convocation

This was the reason why they gathered in Seoul to make a new covenant for justice, peace and the integrity of creation, the statement explained.

The process of discussion and agreement in the convocation was not easy. The participants did not have a common understanding of the difficulties and challenges the global community was facing. One participant called the convocation a wrecked ship. Some participants regretted that the convocation was not capable of guiding the participants to consensus and did not get out of the liberation theology's perspectives. The participants were from all over the world. They were living in different social and political environments, and could not see and understand the difficulties and challenges faced by the global community with same interpretations, perspectives and positions. It was not easy from the beginning to expect the participants to reach an agreement after discussing diverse issues in a limited time. In spite of these difficulties, the convocation could generate a covenant that included four detailed responsibilities of churches. These responsibilities were to act for a just world order and people's liberation from debts, to work for the safety of all countries and peoples, to protect all creatures and share suffering with them, to work for the protection of earth's atmosphere and to pay attention to all people and work for the elimination of racism and discrimination at the national and international levels.

The theological position of the convocation was

articulated by the ten affirmations in the theological document that was adopted at the convocation. The affirmations included the responsibility for the exercise of power as accountable to God, God's option for the poor, the equal value of all races and peoples, male and female as created in the image of God, truth as the foundation of a community of free people, justice as the only foundation of Christ's peace and sustainable peace, God's love for the creation, the earth as the Lord's, the dignity and commitment of the younger generation, and human rights given by God.

These affirmations were the essence of the JPIC theology and meant that churches interpreted the problems of racism, gender discrimination, the third world debt, the global ecological crisis, militarization of the global community and nuclear weapons as the agendas that churches must deal with and respond to with theological perspectives.

On the other hand, church leaders from third world countries shared their stories of discrimination and oppression throughout the convocation. A South African minister shared his own experience of being a victim of discrimination and an aborigine from Australia also shared the aborigine's suffering from the deprivation of land. Most agendas presented for discussions at the convocation were caused by Western superpowers' unjust exercise of power. The participants answered the stories of suffering with one voice asking Christians in Western superpowers to repent. They agreed that the global community could not get out of the crisis of living without

Western superpowers' repentance. All the churches in the world were also requested to repent. Churches and Christians did not take the responsibility of humanity as God's agents of peace and therefore, were requested to repent their sin of avoiding Christ's cross to realize God's kingdom on earth.

The final statement of the JPIC Convocation began with repentance. The participants confessed that they had broken the covenant with God and prayed for God's forgiveness. They emphasized that they were facing a critical moment and it was the time to reaffirm the covenant with God. They confirmed that all the creatures on the earth were suffering from injustice, war and the destruction of God's creation because of their violation of the covenant. They articulated that it was time for all churches and Christians to repent and pray for God's forgiveness. The participants also confirmed their participation in Koreans' struggle for reunification and support for the 1995 Jubilee Campaign with prayers.

The spirit and the confession of the JPIC Convocation have been shared with Christians in Korea and influenced Christians' civil movements including environmental campaigns but have not penetrated enough into individual churches, which are still much more interested in the growth of churches.

Churches' Participation in Politics in the First Republic

30 Nation

"Imagine a world where there is no Christian congressman. Christians would not have any clue how to find people to ask to resolve big or small matters related to churches and church members. The pastors who insist on a distant relationship between church and state should realize this."

This is an editorial from *Christian Newspaper*, which was published during the Rhee Syngman government. This kind of idea is unacceptable now but was possible in the political environment of the time. Christianity was treated like the national religion in the short US military government and the

First Republic of the Rhee Syngman government. Churches therefore could enjoy a lot of privilege. The Constitution articulated the freedom of religion but religious equality was not guaranteed in terms of policies. Churches enjoyed many privileges. Churches could easily obtain real estate that had been abandoned by the Japanese for building churches. Relief supplies from other countries were first transferred to churches and military chaplaincies and prison missions were monopolized by Protestant churches. Churches could run mission programs at the state-run radio station and they facilitated national ceremonies. Churches could correct textbooks that were not favorable to Christianity. The government would accept churches' requests without exception whenever there were important social matters. The US military government and the Rhee Syngman government maintained Japan's regulations against Buddhist and Confucian facilities and suppressed these religions. The government's preferential treatment of churches was obvious and visible. Churches maintained a close relationship with politicians. Lee Giboong, who held various high-ranking positions in the Rhee Syngman government, donated one million won for Methodist pastors' travel and helped the Methodist Church find a building site in Gwanghwamoon which was the center of Seoul. Because of its relationship with President Rhee Syngman, the YMCA was able to make a construction fund by forcing congressmen to donate five percent of their salaries.

Churches actively participated in politics to maintain the Christian-friendly political environment and enjoy benefits. The most visible thing was churches' participation in elections. In 1948, church organizations, including the Presbyterian Church of Korea, the NCCK and Christian youth organizations put their own candidates up for the constitutional congress. Eight Christian candidates were elected. In the second congressional election two Christian candidates were elected. Christians occupied major high-ranking positions in public agencies, in the US military government and in the Rhee Syngman government. Thirty-five out of fifty high-ranking officials were Christians in the US military government in 1946. This rate was too high considering that the Christian population was only 0.52 percent at that time. There were thirteen ordained pastors in the 198-member congress. Nine Christians(two of them were ordained pastors) joined the twenty one-member cabinet. In the Rhee Syngman government, Christians occupied forty percent of high-ranking positions in public agencies and more than forty-seven percent of positions in the cabinet.

Churches' involvement in elections was very organized. Church leaders organized an ad hoc group for the first congressional election in 1948. The NCCK organized the Christian Election Committee for the presidential election in 1952. This committee opened local branches in provinces, counties and local churches to support Rhee Syngman. The NCCK also organized an election committee for the general election in 1954 and decided to screen candidates. In 1956, some Christians raised questions about churches' direct participation in the politics saying "churches must not be political organizations," and "churches must not support or be used by specific parties." Church organizations did not officially organize election committees at this time. But some church leaders privately organized a Christian committee and supported Rhee Syngman, the candidate for the presidency and his running mate Lee Giboong. The chair and two vice chairs of this committee had high positions in the NCCK, one Christian organization still deeply involved in elections. Methodist churches were more directly involved in the election campaign because Rhee Syngman and Lee Gibbong were Methodists. Chungdong First Methodist Church assigned Rhee Syngman to elder and officially supported his third term. The Central District also announced a statement requesting Rhee Syngman's candidacy.

Churches maintained personal relationships with political and high-ranking officials. The NCCK hosted a reception for congressmen in Chungdong First Methodist Church on July 17, 1948 when the Constitution was declared. On August 19, 1952, the NCCK organized the Christian Political Committee and decided to apply Christian ideas to policies. On June 25, 1952, thirty-nine Christian congressmen of the ruling Liberal Party organized the Christian Congressmen Fellowship with the ultimate goal of working in the Congress as a bargaining body. Churches and Christian newspapers supported this idea. The official newspaper of the Presbyterian Church of Korea supported this idea, later urging Christian congressmen to organize a bargaining body to work for church growth in an editorial in 1954. In 1958, this newspaper reported about the elected

▶ Churches' election campaign poster supporting Rhee Syngman's Liberal Party

Christian congressmen, and it asked them to work and cooperate for the growth and freedom of churches and to support churches in the Congress.

There were different understandings of the political situation in the church when most citizens were angry about the unfair election of March 15, 1960 and protested against the government. Chungdong First Methodist Church sent congratulatory telegraphs to Rhee Syngman and Lee Giboong and had a special Sunday service to celebrate their victories and Rhee Syngman's birthday. Kim Whallan, who had held the post of communication secretary in the Rhee Syngman government, made a remark showing Christians' strong support to Rhee Syngman. After the April 19 Revolution she said at a meeting of university presidents, "the April 19 incident happened because we had not educated students well. Let's go to President Rhee Syngman and apologize for our faults." Citizens were against churches, especially after the April 19 Revolution, because the close relationship between churches and the government was revealed. The Korean Methodist Church and the NCCK had to announce statements and apologize for their inappropriate behaviors. Many Christians regretted and lamented this situation. An editorial in *Christians* showed their despair.

"*Korean churches unfortunately have not fulfilled their duties since independence and have failed to be a good model for citizens. Now churches are even criticized by citizens···bloody conflicts, denominational divisions competing for power and court trials are continuing. Scandals over relief supplies, ugly denominational disputes over funding, degraded pastors' participation in corruption, pro-Japan leaders' and swindlers' control over churches, etc···*"

It looked like all churches maintained a close relationship with the US military government and the Rhee Syngman government and enjoyed a lot of benefit. It was mostly true, but there was also conflict over this kind of political support and benefit within the church. Heungsadan, founded by Ahn Changho, and Dongjiheo, founded by Rhee Syngman in the colonial era, competed with each other to take control over the national right-wing movement and gain absolute power inside the church. Most people in Heungsadan were Presbyterians from the northwest(North Korea now). By contrast, most people in Dongjihoe were Methodists based in the Choongchung area. In the US military government, the Heungsadan group took the controlling power and maintained a cooperative relationship with the Dongjihoe group. But with the inauguration of the Rhee Syngman government, the two groups returned to the old competition. The Christians from the northwest had important positions in the government after the May 16 Coup but they did not have many positions in the cabinet of the Rhee Syngman government. Rhee Syngman considered personal relationships to be the most important and appointed the members of Dongjihoe and his old friends whom he had worked with in the US to the positions in the cabinet. Lee Giboong, Yoon Chiyoung, Lim Youngsin, Lim Byungjik, Huh Jeong, Jang Giyoung, Kim Hyuncheol and Lee Wonsoon were old friends who had built personal relationships with Rhee Syngman in the US. No one from the North Korean area was included. As a result, the Heungsadan group gathered under the anti-Rhee Syngman banner and re-emerged at the center of a new faction that confronted the old faction of the Korea Party and the People's Party until the establishment of the Democratic Party.

Theological Interpretation of Korean Tradition and Experience

Debates on Indigenous Theologies and Minjung Theology

In the 1960s, an effort to build indigenous Korean theologies was made. This effort focused on interpreting and understanding the bible in the context of Korea. Cultural nationalism emerged in the third world countries after the Second World War and many countries started emphasizing nationalistic characteristics of their cultures. Korean theologians were influenced by this new idea and discussed the need for indigenous theologies.

The effort for building indigenous theologies first began by Methodist theologians. Yoo Dongsik and Yoon

Sungbeom who initiated the effort were teaching at the Methodist Theological Seminary. Other theologians who were interested in this effort were mostly affiliated with the Methodist Church. Yoo Dongsik was interested in building a Korean theology after the late 1950s. He presented a direction of the Korean theology arguing that the Orientals must refer to the Confucian term tao(morality) to understand the bible just as the Greeks had chosen the term logos to understand the Jew's Messiah. Jeon Kyungyeon refuted Yoo Dongsik's argument. He asserted that the Korean churches needed not the indigenous interpretation of the bible but the indigenous culture of Christianity. He emphasized that the tradition and confession of Western churches must be transplanted with the introduction of Christianity to Oriental societies. Other theologians presented their own ideas as the debate between the two theologians continued. Lee Jangsik, a church historian, criticized Jeon Kyungyeon's position and Lee Gyuho, a philosopher, also supported Yoo Dongsik's argument.

In the same period, there was a similar debate going on between Yoon Sungbeom and Park Bongrang. The debate between Yoo Dongsik and Jeon Kyungyeon was rather abstract, focusing on the need for indigenous interpretation of the bible and indigenous methods of interpretation. But the debate between Yoon Sungbeom and Park Bongrang was about the interpretation of the Tangun mythology.* Yoon Sungbeom

* Tangun is considered to be the founding father of the Korean people.

bravely argued that the three characters, Whanin, Whanwoong and Whangeom(Tangun) in the Tangun mythology were God and this idea of the three gods had been influenced by the idea of the Trinity. Park Bongrang refuted Yoon Sungbeom's interpretation and argued that there was no relation between the Trinity of Christianity and the three gods of the Tangun mythology. He asserted that Korean ethnic culture, tradition and mythology were not connected with Christian revelation and the bible was the only source of Christian revelation. This debate proceeded through the famous magazine *Sasanggye*(meaning a world of ideology) and caught the attention of a huge audience in cultural and academic fields.

Yoon Sungbeom and Yoo Dongsik continued their studies of indigenous theologies in an independent way. Yoon Sungbeom invented the conceptions of 'gam'(sense), 'somssi'(skill) and 'meot'(flavor) and presented a framework of the Korean method of theological studies based on these conceptions in *Christianity and Korean Ideology*(1964). In the 1970s, he presented an indigenous theology called 'Theology of Seong.' Seong comes from a Chinese character comprised of two characters, 'eon'(word) and 'seong'(achievement) and has the meaning of devotion. He explained that 'seong,' which is found in Confucian books and also Yulgok's ideology,* was connected to the passage "the Word became flesh(John 1:14)." In response to

---

* Yulgok(1536–1584) was one of the prominent Confucian scholars in the Yi Dynasty.

this argument, Lee Jongseong who was one of the prominent theologians of the Presbyterian church criticized Yoon Sungbeom and called his theology a syncretism. Kim Uiwhan recommended that Yoon Sunbeom focus not on the development of an indigenous theology but on the authentic interpretation of the bible.

Yoo Dongsik explained the influence of Confucianism, Buddhism and Buddhist doctrines on Koreans' mentality and presented a direction for the development of indigenous theologies in *Korean Religions and Christianity*(1965). In the 1970s, he concentrated on the study of shamanism. He argued that shamanism was the foundation of Korean culture and greatly influenced Christianity in Korea together with Confucianism, Buddhism and Buddhist doctrines. In the 1980s, he asserted that 'Poongryu'(elegance) was the origin of Korean ideologies and could be the basis of indigenous theologies. Byeon Seonwhan, a professor of the Methodist Theological Seminary, continued the work of Yoon Sungbeom and Yoo Dongsik. He emphasized inter-faith dialogue with Buddhism for the development of indigenous theologies. He recognized the salvation of other religions and as a result, was deprived of his professorship and clergy status by the leadership of the Methodist Church.

In the 1970s, Minjung(People's) Theology was the most discussed of Korean theologies. Minjung Theology was formed out of churches' involvement in human rights and democratization movements. In the 1920s, Christian socialists and social activists were especially sympathetic with poor people who were victimized by unjust social structures and theological interpretations of this problem. Minjung Theology inherited this tradition and developed deeper theological insight into the Korean context after the 1960s and theologized it in a more theoretical way.

The social background of Minjung Theology was the political and economic context of Korea in the 1970s. At that time, Korean society was suffering from the military dictatorship of the Yushin government and the economic paradox caused by the rapid industrialization. People's survival and human rights were threatened in this situation. Christians shared the reality faced by marginalized people and developed their theological insights into society. This was the foundation of Minjung Theology. Ahn Byungmoo, Suh Namdong, Hyun Younghak, Kim Yongbok and Suh Gwangseon were the core group of this theology. Most of them participated in the anti-dictatorship, pro-democracy movement and as a result, were dismissed or imprisoned at some time. Minjung theologians were actively engaged in exchanges with activists in other areas and often gathered at the Korean Theological Institute, the CISJD(Christian Institute for the Study of Justice and Development) and the Education Institute of the Presbyterian Church of the ROK for discussions and studies.

Suh Namdong emphasized that there could be

no reconciliation between the rich and the poor and the oppressor and the oppressed, and Minjung must be the main subject of theology. He later embraced diverse methods of biblical interpretations based on social studies and presented an independent method of biblical interpretation emphasizing insightful interpretations of the Holy Spirit. According to him, the bible was not an absolute standard but a reference. In this context, he found Minjung Theology's theological agendas at the conjunction of Christianity's popular traditions and the Korean people's traditions.

Ahn Byungmoo was a biblical theologian who deepened Minjung Theology. On March 1, 1975, he made a speech titled "Nation, Minjung and Church" in a ceremony to celebrate the release of activists. He emphasized Minjung as a more fundamental entity than nation. He argued that the oppressor constantly had exploited Minjung in the name of the nation and the struggle of the oppressed had continued throughout human history. He presented a few examples from Korean history such as Hong Kyungrae's Revolt, the Donghak Revolution, the March First Movement and the April 19 Revolution. His argument caught the attention of world churches.

Hyun Younghak found a religiously critical transcendence from the humor of Talchoom* while Suh Namdong

---

* This is a Korean traditional masque dance in which people interpret their reality and suffering with humor.

and Ahn Byungmoo were leading the Minjung Theology movement. Kim Yongbok tried to interpret people's stories of suffering and liberation through people's social stories and Suh Gwangseon worked on revealing the form of the Minjung faith out of shamanism.

The term, Minjung Theology was established in the academic field in the 1970s. Theologians agreed to use the term for an international theology symposium hosted by the NCCK. The presentations made in the symposium were published in a book, *Minjung and Korean Theology*(1982). This book was translated into English and contributed to sharing Minjung Theology with world churches.

In the 1990s, passion for Minjung Theology rapidly decreased. The meaning and social role of Minjung Theology was diminished with the end of the military government and the emergence of the civil movement. In the 21st century, Minjung Theology is still studied by the theologians affiliated with the Korean Association of Minjung Theology and the Minjung Theology Institute but it does not get much social and academic attention compared to that in the past. In spite of this changing situation, Minjung Theology still has an important meaning in terms of its contribution to making a theology of people's suffering in the Korean context in insightful and creative ways.

Human Rights
and Democratization Movements

32 Nation

Park Chunghee was officially inaugurated as the President in December 1963 and tried to normalize the diplomatic relationship with Japan to develop the national economy with Japanese capital. He faced strong opposition from the entire nation. Churches also thought it was too early to forgive Japan and normalize the relationship with Japan. They joined the people's protest. This was a courageous action for churches that had been compromising with the political sector for a long time. Nevertheless, Park Chunghee signed the Korea–Japan Agreement in June 1965. Church leaders including Gang Shinmyung, Gang Wonyong, Kim Jaejoon and Han Kyungjik gathered at Younglak Church and announced a statement with their prayers for the nation. In the statement, they rejected subordination to all impure and inferior external powers and expressed their strong protest against all forms of dictatorship, injustice and corruption. This stimulated churches across the country and prayer meetings were organized to oppose the humiliating Korea-Japan Agreement.

Park Chunghee tried to amend the constitution for his third term in 1969 and ecumenical church leaders including Kim Jaejoon, Ham Seokheon and Park Hyungyu participated in and led the people's opposition campaign. Kim Jaejoon took the position of the campaign's chair. The NCCK announced a statement in September and expressed its opposition to the amendment. On the other hand, conservative church leaders including Kim Yoonchan, Kim Joongon and Kim Jangwhan criticized Kim Jaejoon's participation in the opposition campaign as the abuse of his clergy power. They rather urged Christians to pray for the President. A Christian association was organized in a hurry and announced a statement welcoming Park Chunghee's courageous decision and the amendment for his third term. The amendment eventually succeeded.

In December 1972, the Park Chunghee government announced the Yushin Constitution and built the foundation of Park Chunghee's long-term authoritarian control over the country. Most churches supported the government actively or silently. But many Christians strongly opposed the

Yushin government. The Namsan Easter Worship Incident and the Korea Christian Statement in 1973 were good examples of Christians' protest. A group of Christians had a worship service on Easter morning at Namsan and distributed anti-government leaflets. This was the Namsan Easter Worship Incident. Park Hyunggyu, the members of the Korea Student Christian Federation and Christian activists working for the poor were arrested under the charge of conspiracy of a rebellion. This arrest became the beginning of consecutive prayers and street demonstrations. For example, 250 students from Seoul National University demonstrated in front of the April 19 Memorial Tower asking for a liberal, democratic society.

The NCCK announced the Human Rights Statement in November 1972 as the government's violations of human rights were getting serious. This statement urged churches to participate in the protection of human rights and to struggle together with the people. This statement was a big support to civil organizations that could not find the support of the general public. This became an opportunity for churches to build a working relationship with civil organizations for collaboration and solidarity.

In January 1974, the first and the second emergency laws were declared. The NCCK had prayer meetings for the nation and urged the government to withdraw the emergency laws and abolish the Yushin Constitution. But the government's oppression and violation of human rights were getting crueler. The government eventually fabricated the Mincheonghakryeon Incident and arrested and indicted 180 students, accusing them of being anti-government communists. The NCCK established the Human Rights Committee in May based on respect for human rights found in the biblical faith. The committee organized Thursday prayers and the member denominations of the NCCK announced statements concerning the country's political situation. In September 1974, the 59th General Assembly of the Presbyterian Church of the ROK announced a statement and the 59th General Assembly of the Presbyterian Church of Korea also announced a statement. The General Conference of the Korean Methodist Church announced a statement in December. In November of the same year, sixty six progressive theologians announced the Korean Christians' Theological Statement and supported churches' participation in the human rights and democratization movements.

The cruel Yushin government could not perfectly muzzle churches. The leaders of the Protestant and Catholic churches announced a statement for the nation together with opposition leaders on March 1, 1976. The statement was announced at the ceremonial worship commemorating the March First Movement and asked for the withdrawal of the emergency laws, the abolition of the Yushin Constitution and the resignation of Park Chunghee. The government labeled this as a plot to overthrow the government and immediately arrested twenty leading figures including Ham Sewoong, Moon Jeonghyun and Kim Seonghoon from the Catholic church and Ham Seokheon,

Moon Ikwhan, Ahn Byungmoo and Lee Woojeong from the Protestant church. Many political figures including Kim Daejung, Yoon Bosun and Chung Ilhyung were involved in this incident as well as many Catholic and Protestant church leaders. This incident therefore caught the attention of many, domestically and internationally.

The international ecumenical movement supported the Korean progressive churches' democratization movement. One of the biggest supporters was the WCC. Its member churches in Germany, the US and Japan also paid close attention to human right issues in Korea. In April 1975, Kim Gwansuk, the general secretary of the NCCK, Cho Seunghyuk and Park Hyunggyu were arrested under the charge of breach of trust. This was a shocking event for world churches. The Commission on World Mission and Evangelism of the WCC held an extraordinary meeting in Geneva in November 1975 and

▶ Human Rights Week Worship in 1975

discussed measures to support Korean churches' human rights and democratization movements. In this meeting, a group to connect world churches to Korean churches' social movements was organized. This group was a strong support to the democratization and reunification movements until the 1980s.

In 1980, Chun Doohwan ordered the Gwangju Massacre* when he gained power. He maintained a tight control over all social sectors and severely oppressed the democratization movement. Churches kept seeking a new way of social participation in this harsh political environment. The NCCK Human Rights Committee, the Korean Student Christian Federation, the Ecumenical Youth Council in Korea and the Urban Industrial Mission maintained their strong support to and

* This was named the Gwangju Democratic Uprising after the government's recognition of people's suffering and uprising in 1996.

active involvement in social movements. New church organizations including the National Clergy Conference for Justice and Peace, the Christian Farmers' Association, the Christian Workers' Association and the Korean Association of Christian Women for Women Minjung emerged and expanded the boundary of Christian social movements. These new Christian organizations based in the field vitalized Christian activism. In the mid-1980s these organizations led diverse Christian movements relating to peace and reunification, and the education of democratic citizens and the social movements of Christian students, youth, farmers and women.

Around 1984, Minjung churches emerged. These churches rooted in Minjung Theology emerged in the process of churches' involvement in human rights and democratization issues and urban industrial missions in the 1970s. They became an axis of Christians' social reform

▶ Human Rights Week worship in 1981

movements. The number of Minjung churches reached ninety in 1989. The YMCA, which had been inactive since the country's independence, restored its spirit of activism and cultivated its involvement in social movements. The National Clergy Conference for Justice and Peace introduced Christian social movements to church pastors through its members. This organization was founded in July 1984 by a few progressive pastors who were interested in analyzing and examining the suffering of churches and society, and taking concrete actions. This organization worked closely with the NCCK and played a leading role in the democratization and peace and reunification movements.

The Korean Association of Evangelism was founded by conservative pastors and theologians in 1981. This organization announced a statement on their position regarding the political situation in May 1986. This statement showed that the political position of conservative Christians who had been arguing for the separation of religion from politics and who were silent regarding political issues was changing. This change became more obvious after the June Uprising* in 1987. The Evangelical Christian Student Association was organized in November 1987 to watch the fair presidential election and the

---

* This anti-dictatorship, pro-democracy protest occurred from June 10 to 29. The torture of Park Jongcheol and his death in prison and Lee Hanyeol's death by the police use of tear gas lit the fuse of mass demonstrations all over the country. The uprising reached its climax on June 10 and continued until June 29. President Roh Taewoo gave in to the people's resistance and announced the constitutional amendment for a direct presidential election. The first presidential election based on this amendment took place on December 16, 1987.

establishment of a democratic government. The Evangelical Youth Association was organized in March 1988 and the Christian Ethics Movement of Korea was founded at this time to emphasize Christian ethics and respond to social issues.

Missions to Change Inhumane Working Conditions
Urban Industrial Missions

33 Nation

In the 1960s, Korean society experienced a rapid industrialization and urbanization. The rapid change of society caused many social problems and churches became interested in missions for marginalized people. Urban industrial missions began in this context.

The urban industrial missions began with the momentum of Henry Jones's visit to Korea in March 1957. Jones was in charge of the Asia Desk of the US United Presbyterian Church's Global Missions. The Presbyterian Church of Korea established the Committee of Industrial Missions and began industrial missions in Youngdeongpo, Seoul in 1958. In November 1957, the Catholic Church also organized a Catholic young workers' group called J.O.C.(Jeunesse Ouvrière Chretiènne) to focus on salvation in the working class. In 1961, the Korean Methodist Church began industrial missions in Incheon and the Anglican Church of Korea in Hwangji in Gangwon-do. The Presbyterian Church of the ROK(1963), the Salvation Army(1965) and the Korean Evangelical Church(1973) followed the other churches' initiatives. In the early years the industrial missions did not go beyond traditional missions for workers. Most programs focused on religious trainings for lay people, worship for workers, bible studies, literal missions and free time activities. These were not different from traditional programs in the church.

In the 1960s, people with professional knowledge joined churches' industrial missions and church organizations' programs for workers changed. The program staff would work in the field with factory workers for six to twelve months before their involvement in industrial missions. They would experience the gap between the church and the working class. They realized that industrial missions must deal with the matters and problems that were regarded as life issues in the field. They therefore discussed the issues of wages, working conditions, unions, safety and layoffs, and tried to reinterpret the issues in terms of the bible. They also made new programs that were totally different from traditional church activities such as training programs for union leaders and support to the organization of unions. It was especially remarkable that they could make progress and no longer limit the training programs to union leaders, but start workers' schools for union members. They changed the name for their work from industrial evangelism to urban industrial missions(UIM) in 1968.

But the situation of workers was formidable. The political sector chose to pursue export-oriented economic development based on low wages and the business sector enormously benefited from this policy. Workers had to endure horrible working conditions, inhumane treatments and extremely low wages. Workers had to work like machines. On November 13, 1970, Jeon Taeil, a young worker in the Pyeonghwa Market, burned himself to reveal the inhumane working conditions to the nation. This was a shocking incident to Korean society and encouraged the public to pay attention to labor problems. But the government had no interest in improving working conditions and

▶Staff of the Youngdeungpo Urban Industrial Mission in its early years

rather isolated workers' voices from society to accomplish its goal of economic development and to show the world that the country was politically stable. The government criticized and suppressed church organizations engaged in urban industrial missions. Even the Federation of Korean Trade Unions and other individual industrial unions were pro-government and therefore, in conflict with these church organizations.

On the other hand, many churches were constantly growing and strengthening their support to the government. These churches were very critical about the church organizations engaged in not industrial evangelism but industrial missions for workers. They considered churches' ignorance of spreading the gospel and concentration on social issues as churches' deviation from Christian faith. But the organization of urban industrial missions strengthened the theology of urban industrial missions in terms of the WCC's concept of the 'Mission

▶ Holy Communion with workers at Youngdeungpo Labor Church (now Seongmoonbak Church)

of God(Missio Dei).' They considered Korean churches' missions that concentrated on individuals' spiritual salvation to be ignorant of Korean society's structural problems and the miserable reality of workers. They believed that the structural problems that were destroying people's lives must be eliminated first to save individuals, communities and society as a whole. In this context, the conflict between conservative churches and the organizations working on urban industrial missions escalated.

In the 1970s, the organizations working on urban industrial missions became the only places for union workers to get some practical help. These workers were excluded from society and could not even get attention from mainline churches. These organizations were rare groups that were interested in workers' issues and especially in women workers' issues at that time. This was an important signpost in the history of Christian missions.

The more the organizations engaged in urban industrial missions spoke for workers the more the government suppressed these organizations. The government labeled these organizations as communist groups that penetrated within unions and promoted class struggle, and tried isolate them from churches and society. In 1978, Dongil Union Incident* occurred

---

* This was a women workers' strike protesting against low wages and the company's suppression of their union. The government intervened in this strike to support the company as the strike continued and intruded into a union meeting and poured human feces over the women workers.

and the Incheon Urban Industrial Mission was involved in the incident. The urban industrial mission organizations announced a theological statement expressing their firm position on urban industrial missions and support to the union. In the statement they articulated that the urban industrial mission was resulted from the structural problem that ignored unjust, inhumane working conditions, and their work was an effort to correct the problem based on the biblical teaching of the good Samaritan. Other church organizations and Christian women's groups organized an ad hock committee and actively responded to the incident. In 1979, YH Union Strike* occurred. The government accused the urban industrial mission organizations related to the union and arrested the organizations' staff. The NCCK strongly supported the union's struggle and the organizations saying "the protection of workers' human rights was one of churches' duties given by God." It articulated that the urban industrial mission was the expansion of churches' work. The General Assembly of the Presbyterian Church of Korea in 1980 stated that "the urban industrial mission was inevitable in industrialized Korean society."

The urban industrial mission continued in the 1980s. But workers were now more capable of organizing themselves and the role and work of church organizations

---

* The YH union started a strike protesting against the company's abrupt, unilateral closing of its factory. The union members occupied the opposition party's office and the government violently stopped the protest by sending 2,000 policemen. A woman worker died during the police operation.

reduced. However, these organizations maintained their interest in industrialized society and workers. In the changing environment, churches have been focusing on labor rights and the working conditions of migrant foreign workers and irregular Korean workers.

Minjung, the Center of Reunification

Christian Reunification Movement

34 Nation

After the Korean War, South Korea considered North Korea not as a dialogue and negotiation partner but as an enemy to destroy. Churches basically shared this idea. Churches considered their role in reunification as that of a Christian army that could liberate North Koreans. They understood that North Korea was ruled by evil and they had a duty to liberate North Koreans who were oppressed and starving under the authoritarian regime. This was the Christian version of the anti-communist reunification ideology. At this time, there was no big ideological difference between conservative and progressive churches.

The July 4 South-North Joint Statement was signed in 1972 and churches had an opportunity to reflect on their ignorance about national reunification and their compliance with the national divide. Churches started to pay attention to reunification issues. The NCCK organized the Christian Association for Reunification and Social Justice in October 1972. This association expressed the progressive Christians' position on reunification. This position was based on two major ideas. First, a peaceful reunification could not be achieved without true democratization in South Korea. It meant that South Korea's democratization, freedom, human rights and social justice should be the foundation of a peaceful victory over North Korea. Secondly, government-led discussions on reunification should end and different groups of people could participate in the discussion. It meant that the Minjung must lead the discussion.

In the 1970s, progressive church leaders confronted Park Chunghee's dictatorship and constantly engaged in resistance. But Park Chunghee's Yushin government oppressed the democratization movement on the grounds of the country's industrialization and national security. In this situation, progressive church leaders came to the conclusion that the national divide that legitimized national security must be first overcome by democratization. However, it took a long time for churches to take systemic and activism-oriented approaches to reunification issues at this time.

The Yushin government ended with the

October 26 Incident* in 1979 but the 'spring of democratization' had not yet come. A new military government began with the December 12 Coup. This government was more oppressive and ordered the Gwangju Massacre in May 1980. The international community became interested in human rights issues in Korea after the Gwangju Massacre. The NCCK and progressive churches realized a need for building a close relationship and solidarity with the WCC and world churches to reveal and eradicate the military government's human rights violations and inhumane treatments of people. The political slogan of the new military government followed the line of the Yushin government, emphasizing national security. The churches' solidarity work with world churches naturally focused on reunification issues that were regarded as the root of the government's oppression and all political problems.

In June 1981, churches held the fourth Korea-Germany Church Council at Academy House with the theme, "the confession of sin and a new responsibility.' This was a new beginning for churches to deal with reunification issues actively. After this event, Korean Christians living abroad met North Koreans in Vienna(November 1981) and Helsinki(December 1981). The NCCK organized the Council for Reunification in 1983. But it could not even hold a meeting due to the government's

* This incident ended Park Chunghee's eighteen-year dictatorship. Park Chunghee was assassinated by the head of the Central Intelligence Agency in a safe house on October 26.

interference. The government arrested thirteen staffers of CISJD(Christian Institute for the Study of Justice and Development) who were working on the publication of a reunification textbook. In this oppressive domestic environment churches had to approach reunification issues and take action in solidarity with world churches and with Koreans abroad who were free from the Korean government's interference.

Korean churches and world churches shared the understanding that the divide of the Korean peninsula was the root cause of the anti-democratic and anti-human rights Korean situation. They also shared that the Korean situation was threatening world peace and Christians in the world must make efforts for reunification on the Korean peninsula. Churches in Korea could have a clearer direction for the reunification movement in solidarity with world churches. The most important event that contributed to this direction was the Conference on Peace and Justice in Northeast Asia, the so-called Tozanso Conference, held in Tozanso nearby Tokyo from October 29 to November 2, 1984. This conference was hosted by the WCC-CCIA(Commission of the Churches on International Affairs). It showed the ecumenical movement's interest in and work for peace and justice in Northeast Asia. The WCC-CCIA organized the conference in close contact and consultation with the CCA(Christian Conference of Asia), the NCCJ(National Christian Council in Japan), the NCCK and the WCC member churches in Korea. The WCC-CCIA invited Christian representatives of North Korea and China to the conference. However, the political situation in Korea was not favorable and most Korean churches had a fundamental question about the existence of churches in North Korea. The NCCK and Korean delegates could not ignore this fact. The North Korean and Chinese churches rejected the invitation and the historical meeting between the South Korean and North Korean churches was postponed to the next meeting.

This conference was the first official international meeting for Korean churches and world churches to deal with peace and reunification issues in the Korean peninsula in public, and it made a great contribution to the Korean churches' reunification movement by providing a turning point. The conference generated the so-called Tozanso Report that contained prospects for the peaceful resolution of conflict. This report had a significant influence on Korean churches in designing the direction of the reunification movement. The report had three main suggestions. First, justice and peace should not be separated and must be accomplished together. Secondly, churches in North Korea and South Korea must meet and have dialogues to overcome the national divide and build a mutual trust. Thirdly, the participation of world churches must be promoted for peace in Asia. The meeting between South Korean and North Korean churches was not possible without the support and cooperation of world churches considering the political obstacles and divide of Korea. This practical obstacle encouraged Korean churches abroad that had more possibilities than churches inside Korea to take up reunification issues as one of their priorities and to work for the meeting of churches of the two Koreas.

The NCCK 34th General Assembly announced the Korean Churches' Statement on Peace and Reunification in March 1985. This statement articulated that "the wish for reunification is the reality for the weak, the poor, the oppressed and the Minjung who are in deep despair." It emphasized that the Minjung must be the center of reunification movement and the social reform and the accomplishment of reunification were not separated. The statement of confession announced in the 71st General Assembly of the Presbyterian Church of Korea included churches' duty for peace and reunification in the Korean peninsula.

On February 29, 1988, the NCCK announced the Korean Churches' Statement on Peace and Reunification of the Korea Peninsula(the 88 Statement). In this statement churches first confessed that they had committed a sin by hating North Koreans in the divided structure of the Korean peninsula. It added the principles of humanitarianism and people's democratic participation to the three principles of self-reliance, peace and national cooperation of the July 4 South-North Joint Statement signed by the two Koreas in 1972. These five principles were the conclusion of progressive church leaders' discussions on reunification after 1960. One of the most significant points of the statement was churches' argument for the withdrawal of the US military and reduction of arms in Korea under the condition that neighboring countries should guarantee the establishment of a peaceful political structure in the Korean peninsula. The withdrawal of the US military was a very sensitive issue because North Korea also argued for this. In spite of this controversy, this statement was recognized as a significant document that led the discussion on reunification in Korean society from that time forward.

Conservative churches strongly criticized the statement. Conservative church organizations such as the Korean Council of Evangelism and the Korean Council of Protestant Churches announced statements that opposed the NCCK statement. They strongly disagreed with and rejected the nationalistic optimism, the omnipotent reunification theory, South Korea's responsibility for the national divide, the withdrawal of the US military and the unilateralism of the ecumenical movement. It was a fairly natural response considering that the political position of conservative churches was based on anti-communism and national security.

The reunification movement continued

▶ World Christian Conference on Peace and Reunification of the Korean Peninsula in 1988

although there was strong protest against it by conservative churches. In March 1988, the NCCK hosted the World Conference on Peace and Reunification of the Korean Peninsula in Incheon in cooperation with the WCC-CCIA. The participants in this conference supported the 88 Statement and requested that the UN make an effort to solve the problem of divided families on the Korean peninsula. They also articulated that military drills should be immediately stopped and nuclear weapons should be eliminated to ease the political tension between the two Koreas and accomplish reunification. This discussion on reunification influenced the government's announcement of reunification policies in the July 7 Statement in 1988.

The reunification movement of churches made a big contribution to the opening of South-North exchanges at the private level. In September 1986, The WCC-CCIA hosted the first Glion Meeting in Switzerland and arranged a meeting between South and North Korean Christians. This was a historical event that Christians from the two Koreas met for the first time. The second Glion Meeting was held in November 1988 and South and North Korean Christians met again. The representatives of the two Korean churches announced the Glion Statement together. In the statement, the representatives declared the year 1995(which would be the 50th anniversary of Korea's independence) as the Jubilee of Reunification. They agreed to observe the Common Sunday for Reunification every year on Sunday immediately before the Independence Day on August 15. They reconfirmed the three principles of national reunification from the July 4 South-North Joint Statement and that the Minjung should stand at the center of the reunification movement. They urged the two Korean governments to cut armaments in order to build mutual trust and ease tension on the Korean peninsula. This statement was significant because it was the first South-North statement at the non-government level.

In March 1989, Rev. Moon Ikhwan visited North Korea. He joined the Easter Worship at Bongsu Church in Pyongyang and met Kim Il Sung, the head of North Korea. He shared his ideas about reunification with the North Korean leader. In January 1992, Kwon Hokyung, the general secretary of the NCCK, and Park Kyungseo, who was in charge of the Asia Desk of the WCC, visited North Korea at the invitation of the Korean Christian Federation in North Korea and met Kim Il Sung. They invited the delegation of the Korean Christian Federation to the NCCK General Assembly in 1992. The representatives of the two Korean churches later met at

▶ Meeting of South and North Korean Churches in 1992

Panmunjom and discussed detailed plans for the North Korean Christians' visit. But the visit was not realized due to the South Korean government's interference at the last minute.

In 1993, churches were expecting the Jubilee of Reunification that had been agreed by the two Korean churches at the second Glion Meeting. The NCCK organized the Human Chain at Imjingak located in South Korea just outside the DMZ(demilitarized zone). This was a big public event with the participation of 65,000 Christians and citizens on August 15, 1993. This was a symbolic event for the churches' reunification movement, which had been emphasizing the central role of the Minjung in reunification.

The Christian reunification movement was led by progressive church leaders and the member denominations of the NCCK. There was constant criticism from conservative churches about the responsibility for the national divide, emotional omnipotence reunification theory, the unilateralism of reunification discussions and tolerance of North Korea's political system, as they would describe it. But the churches' reunification movement led by progressive churches had a significant meaning in terms of attracting society's attention to peace and reunification issues, articulating the central role of the Minjung for reunification and sharing reunification issues with the world community and neighboring countries through the collaboration with the WCC and world churches, and it increased people's understanding of reunification issues.

Prayers to Overcome Despair

Thursday Prayers for the Oppressed

35 Nation

On November 30, 1970 a twenty–two–year–old man, Chun Taeil, burned himself on the street in front of the Pyeonghwa Market in Seoul. He cried out until the last minute of his life, "observe the Labor Standard Law" and "we are not machines."

Chun Taeil's death revealed the huge contradiction of Korean society relating to poor working conditions, the Park Chunghee government's oppression and the problems of export–oriented economic policies. The democratization movement was spread all over the country with this momentum. Many intellectuals and students were arrested and human rights violations increased. The NCCK took human rights issues up as one of its major agendas. On November 23–24, 1973, the NCCK hosted a human rights conference with the theme 'faith and human rights' at Boondo Building in Jangchoong-dong, Seoul. The participants in this conference pointed out human rights violations relating to the Namsan Easter Worship Incident(April 22, 1973) and the demonstration of the Seoul National University students(October 2, 1973). They expressed deep concerns about the increasing cases of human rights violations with the increase of protests against the Yushin government. They confirmed the need for a standing body that could deal with human rights issues in the church and contribute to improving the human rights situation. They suggested the NCCK to establish a human rights committee. On December 10, 1972, the Executive Committee of the NCCK decided to accept the suggestion and establish a standing human rights committee.

On May 4, 1974 the Human Rights Committee of the NCCK began with the commitment to protect human rights and eradicate human rights violations based on the biblical teaching of respecting human dignity. The first officers were Lee Haeyoung, the chair, Lee Taeyoung, the vice chair, and Hong Choongnam, the clerk.

The most urgent agenda for the Human Rights Committee was to respond to the arrest of Rev. Park Hyunggyu during the Namsan Easter Worship Incident and to express the churches' position on the Mincheonghakryun Incident and to take action. The prosecutors of the Emergency Court Martial regarded the Mincheonghakryun as an anti-government group benefiting North Korea and indicted fifty one people on May 27, 1974. The prosecution announced that a group of anti-government students had made plans to overthrow the government and organize nationwide demonstrations. According to the prosecution, they had built cooperative relationships with underground pro-communist groups such as Inhyeokdang, pro-North Korea Korean-Japanese groups, anti-communist groups, anti-government figures and anti-government groups in the church and tried to establish a communist government. There were Christian students working for the Korea Student Christian Federation(KSCF) among the indicted. All leaders of the KSCF including Suh Changseok, the president, and Lee Jikhyung, Ahn Jaewoong and Jung Sangbok were arrested. The Christian student movement was in crisis at this time.

The prosecution finally ruled that Mincheonghakryun was a home-grown communist group engaged in anti-government activities and demanded fifteen to twenty years of imprisonment, a life sentence or even a death sentence for the indicted. But the prosecution's use of torture during the investigation and the fabrication of the incident were revealed in the court. The Park Chunghee government had to face criticism and protest domestically and internationally. In this situation, young pastors affiliated with the Korean Methodist Church, the Presbyterian Church of Korea, the Presbyterian

Church of the ROK, the Korean Holiness Church and the Korean Evangelical Church began gathering at the chapel of the Christian Building in Jongno 5-ga. They regularly gathered on Thursdays. They wanted to share the suffering of the people arrested during the Mincheonghakryun Incident and they prayed together for the arrested and their families. This was the beginning of the Thursday Prayer. It was not intended to include the general public or designed with political intentions. Those young pastors only wanted to pray for suffering people. At the beginning fifteen to twenty pastors participated in the prayer and then the families of the arrested people started to join. The prayer took place regularly at 10 a.m. on every Thursday. The participants increased to hundreds of people before long and the prayer had to move from a small chapel to a big hall. The families who had participated in the prayer later organized their own organization, the Association of Families of the Arrested.

The Thursday Prayer was the only public place

▶ Thursday Prayer

for participants to talk about human rights issues and pray together with others. Families of arrested people, pastors, lay people and non-Christians all together shared their own experiences and people's stories of suffering. It was a place of solidarity for all of them to pray together and make up their minds to struggle for human rights issues.

The government started suppressing the Thursday Prayer as many incidents fabricated by the government were revealed there and more people used the prayer as a place of communication and solidarity for democratization and human rights. The Christian Building and individual churches gave in to the government's pressure and did not open their facilities to the Thursday Prayer. People would gather in private houses and the NCCK office, and they eventually suspended the prayer on May 13, 1975 under the 9th Emergency Law. In the meantime, a few pastors were arrested in relation to the Metropolitan Urban Mission Committee Incident.* People gathered again to pray for these pastors on May 30 and had a prayer meeting on their trial days. The Thursday Prayer resumed on September 18 after the end of the first trial. In 1976, some leaders of the democratization movement announced the March First Statement on Democratization and were arrested. After this incident the NCCK

---

* The government arrested Park Hyunggyu, Kim Gwansuk, Kwon Hokyung and Cho Seunghyuk under the charge of breach of trust. The government found that these pastors had used part of the funding from an international organization to help the families of arrested people and pay for education programs. They were accused of embezzlement.

▶Thursday Prayer

decided to host the prayer at the Christian Building. The NCCK changed the prayer day to Friday on May 3 because trials would hold on Saturday. The NCCK wanted to bring people together to pray for arrested people before trials. The prayer suspended after the 1990s with the country's democratization.

The Thursday Prayer in the 1970s and 1980s was like a feast of prayer. Oppressed and suffering people came together and prayed for one another. They discussed the ways to solve their problems with churches and were encouraged by other participants. The rich and the poor, and the educated and the uneducated, Christians and non-Christians gathered together and cried together. They sometimes hugged and danced together with joy. Churches and people made history together every Thursday.

The Close Relationship between Churches
and the Military Government

The National Prayer Breakfast Meeting

////////////////////////////

36 Nation

Most Christians supported anti-communism when Korea became independent from the Japanese colonial rule in 1945. This anti-communism already penetrated into people's minds during the colonial era. After independence, church leaders did not argue for separation of church and state anymore. Rather, they became involved in politics in a more direct way with the excuse of contributing to building a new country.

Churches' involvement in politics became more visible with the inauguration of President Rhee Syngman who was then a Methodist elder. He opened the constitutional congress with a prayer although there was no prayer in the ceremonial order. He chose a Christian ceremony for his inauguration. It was not legally acceptable in a country that did not have any national religion. Churches enjoyed a variety of benefits regardless of denomination after his inauguration and became intoxicated with political power.

Churches were pushed to the periphery in the political turmoil after the April 19 Revolution and the May 16 Coup. Christians were not at the center of politics any more at this time. But churches still maintained their political legacy of anti-communism and their pro-US position. The Park Chunghee government, which had gained the power through the May 16 Coup, shared these political leanings with the churches.

The relationship between churches and the Park Chunghee government began around 1965 when the country was facing strong protest by the people against the Korea-Japan dialogue. 215 church leaders including Kim Jaejoon, Han Kyungjik, Ham Seokheon, Gang Sinmyung and Gang Wonyong announced their opposition to the restoration of Korea-Japan diplomatic relations in July 1965. This event contributed to spreading churches' protests to major local cities such as Daejeon, Gunsan, Iri, Gwangju and Busan. All churches regardless of their conservative or liberal backgrounds protested against the government's decision. Churches regained the prophetic voice that had played the most important role in leading the people's struggle in the March First Movement.

But churches' positions changed around the Park Chunghee government's dispatch of Korean forces to the Vietnam War. Korea was the first country among the US allies that decided to dispatch a large number of forces to Vietnam. There was no opposition in Korean society where anti-communism was strong. Churches rather strongly supported the government's decision and rationalized that the US had helped Korea during the Korean War, and the decision to dispatch Korean forces was to repay the historical obligation. Churches actively participated in promoting dispatched soldiers' anti-communism and national pride by sending chaplains to the military and even to Vietnam. Churches' active and positive responses to Korea's participation in the Vietnam War supported the government's political intentions. The confrontational relationship between churches and the military government gradually changed to a cooperative relationship based on a common ideological background. The government repaid churches' support with the establishment of police chaplaincies and the permission for prison missions.

The close relationship between churches and the military government officially began with the National Prayer Breakfast Meeting. Rev. Kim Joongon, the founder of the CCC initiated the establishment of this prayer meeting. The CCC was founded by Bill Bright in the US in 1951 and Kim Joongon founded its Korean branch in November 1958. It was the first branch founded after the US one. The founding principles of his CCC were anti-communism and evangelism that emphasized individual salvation based on fundamentalist theology. The CCC and its passionate missions appealed to Christian students in Korea where Christian student movements were weak. The CCC also played an important role in spreading evangelism in the church.

The CCC gradually established itself in Korean society and Kim Joongon planned to introduce the US National Prayer Breakfast to Korea. The US National Prayer Breakfast originated from Christian businessmen's prayer meetings in Seattle in 1935. They would pray together and discuss common agendas. The prayer played an intermediary role that naturally connected Christian businessmen with politicians. Kim Joongon participated in the US National Prayer Breakfast hosted by the Congress in 1963 and 1964. He made plans to hold a national prayer breakfast in Korea and discussed the plan with Robinson who was the general secretary of International Christian Leadership and Halverson who was one of the board members of the International CCC and an advisor to the US National Prayer Breakfast. Kim Joongon gained the support of Park Hyunsook who was a congressman and an elder, and Kim Jongpil who was one of the most powerful figures in the Congress. He held the first National Prayer Breakfast Meeting on February 27, 1965 with the participation of twenty congressmen and politicians including Kim Jongpil, the head of the ruling party, Kim Youngsam, the opposition leader, and Chung Ilkwon, the prime minister. He organized a preparatory committee to hold the prayer meeting regularly and appointed Kim Jongpil, the secretary of the ruling party, and Kim Youngsam, the secretary of the opposition party, to the committee.

Kim Joongon planned to hold the prayer meeting with the presence of the president as was done in the US. Kim Jongpil gained President Park Chunghee's agreement and the CCC eventually hosted the first Presidential National Prayer Breakfast Meeting at Chosun Hotel on March 8, 1966. Robinson and Halverson who had strongly supported Kim Joongon's initiative in Korea were invited together with five members of International Christian Leadership. Ambassadors, including the US Ambassador to Korea, participated in the prayer meeting. High-ranking government officials including Lee Hyosang, the chair of the Congress, and Chung Ilkwon, the prime minister, also participated. Religious leaders including Cardinal Kim Soohwan and Archbishop No Ginam from the Catholic Church, Han Kyungjik, Gang Sinmyung, Yoo Hojoon, Gil Jinkyung(the general secretary of the NCCK) and Kim Whallan from the Protestant church were also invited. Choi Taeseop, the vice chair of the Federation of Korean Industries represented the business sector. Leaders of political, religious and business sectors all joined the prayer meeting but President Park Chunghee who was the leading figure of the event could not participate.

The prominent cultural magazine *Sasanggye* criticized the prayer meeting in its April volume, saying that it had an impure intention betraying the true spirit of Christianity and was simply a political show. But the majority of churches considered the prayer meeting to be non-political and rather supported it. Kim Joongon continued his effort to host the prayer meeting with presence of the president. He could not host the prayer meeting the next year. On May 1, 1968, President Park Chunghee finally joined the prayer meeting and the Presidential National Prayer Breakfast Meeting took place on May 1 every year after that.

Park Chunghee could gain stronger support from church leaders with the continuation of the prayer meeting. He abused the prayer meeting to justify his authoritarian government and policies, and to persuade the international press for his own interests. The 6th Presidential National Prayer Breakfast Meeting in 1973 was the first meeting after the inauguration of the Yushin government in October 1972. Fifty high-ranking officials from fifteen countries were invited to the prayer meeting. The prime minister invited them to a dinner reception that was used to justify the Yushin government. On the other hand, Kim Joongon built a personal relationship with Park Chunghee through the prayer meeting. These two persons sought mutual interests using this personal relationship. One of the examples was the government's financial support for Explo 74, a mega-size mission gathering in Seoul. The prayer meeting did not take place in 1975 after the assassination of First Lady Yook Youngsoo in August 1974. It became called the National Prayer Breakfast Meeting in 1976 and has been continuing until now.

God's World of Life and Peace

Korean Churches' Movement of Life and Peace

In the 1970s, the most serious social problem was poverty. Poverty reduction was a priority for the entire nation and a lot of social energy was put into the effort to overcome poverty. In this context, economic development became the country's top priority. But this choice resulted in the comprehensive degradation of environment. Heavy industries had full support from the government for economic development and emitted an enormous amount of pollutants. The pollutants killed trees and plants and resulted in skin diseases and nerve damage among humans.

Christian organizations such as the Christian Academy, YMCA, YWCA and church women's organizations were the first groups that were interested in the problems of environmental pollution. They hosted seminars on environmental pollution and made efforts to find solutions. In 1982, the Korea Environmental Pollution Institute(now the Christian Association of the Environmental Movement) was founded and environmental pollution was dealt with as a serious social problem. Bread for the World, a German organization, supported this Christian environmental action and annually donated eight million won. That was a big amount of money at that time and the Korea Environmental Pollution Institute, the first environmental organization in Korea, could start its work based on this donation. The environmental movement was initiated by churches in Korea.

The Korea Environmental Pollution Institute suggested celebrating an Environmental Sunday and churches have been observing Environmental Sunday on the first Sunday of June since 1984. The NCCK decided to observe the Sunday in 1990, and as a result, the Environmental Sunday spread to the NCCK member denominations. In 1985, the institute researched pollution-related disease in the Onsan Industrial Area and announced the results. The institute collected samples around the area and sent them to Japan for analyses. The pollution-related disease was cadmium poisoning. All newspapers reported this result in detail and the pollution problem became a social agenda. The pollution issue in the Onsan Industrial Area contributed to

▶ The 7th open seminar of the Korea Environmental Pollution Institute

the stimulus of the environmental movement in Korea. The nuclear power plant incident in Chernobyl also encouraged people to seriously reconsider the safety of nuclear power plant, and as a result, the anti-nuclear movement was formed. The Korea Environmental Pollution Institute played the leading role in advocating about the problem of nuclear plants and, at the same time, encouraged churches to pay attention to nuclear and other environmental issues.

In the late 1990s, there were strong protests against the Dong River and Jiri Mountain dam plans. The government had to give up its large scale construction plans for the first time. Religious leaders and many lay people participated in the protest against the Saemangeum Project.* Moon Gyuhyun, a Catholic priest, Sookyung, a Buddhist monk, Kim Kyungil, a Won Buddhism clergyman and Lee Heewoon, a Protestant pastor marched from Saemangeum in Jeollabuk-do to Seoul. It was not a simple march but a three-step-one-bow march that took them sixty-five days to march 309 kilometers. These religious leaders'

---

* This large scale project was to build a sea dike and reclaim land from the sea in Jeollabuk-do in the southern part of Korea. The construction of the 33.9 kilometer-long sea dike finished in 2010 and 40,100 hectares of land was reclaimed. Many people who were concerned about the destruction of sandbanks, sea ecosystems and people's lives protested for a long time.

march deeply touched people's hearts. Additionally, some big churches expressed their strong support to the project and had special worship services.

God creates, protects and guides life. God wants to create a world where all creatures can live in freedom and peace. But many churches do not participate in protecting life but rather lead the destruction. Churches exist to build a world of life and peace that is God's kingdom. Christians have a duty to follow Christian doctrines that encourage them to witness and share people's sufferings and to transform the world of suffering to a world of life and peace. This is Christ's work that Christians learn from the bible.

God created the world and was pleased. God gave humans a duty to preserve and take care of God's creation. But humans betrayed God and gave in to greed. As a result, natural ecosystems that are the homes of all creatures are in danger. If humans do not change their way of living there is no future for ecosystems or for humanity as well.

In the early 2000s, the tension was high in the Korean peninsula partly due to the US government's dichotomous approaches to world issues and its enemies. The Bush administration pointed out North Korea together with Iran and Iraq as a terror supporting country and called North Korea an axis of evil in 2002 after invading Afghanistan. It was like a warning to North Korea to be prepared for the possibility of a US military operation. The US invaded Iraq in 2003 and many people in Korea were concerned about a possible war in the Korean peninsula. Many religious leaders and concerned people worried about the total destruction of life and peace in the Korean peninsula. A small group of people began the Life and Peace Pilgrimage in Jiri Mountain. They marched across the country for five years and met many people. They greatly contributed to sharing the value of life and peace with the general public. Life and peace are the central values of Christ and therefore, the essence of Christian teachings. Life and peace are also the essence of other religious teachings and in particular, an urgent agenda for people living in this era. Many religious leaders and lay people shared that Korean society must focus on the value of life and peace. This idea became the life and peace movement in Korea.

The government's Four Big Rivers Project* was resisted by most people but the government unilaterally decided to proceed with it. Rivers are traditionally considered to be the basis of life. Religious and civil organizations worried about the destruction of the four rivers, which are major rivers in Korea, and made all efforts to stop the project. These organizations began a pilgrimage to the rivers and shared their

---

* This was the Lee Myungbak government's large scale project to alter the courses of four big rivers by building dams and reservoirs, and clearing river basins. This project began in 2008 and ended in 2012, in a remarkably short time considering the size of the project. It has already caused a lot of environmental and agricultural problems in surrounding areas.

idea with the general public. Religious leaders from five religions walked, ate and prayed together for one hundred days. It was a historical event that brought different religious leaders together to deal with and respond to a life and peace issue. This campaign set the course for other campaigns dealing with the problems of nuclear power plants and increasing golf courses, both affecting the environment and people's lives. In December 2007, 78,918 barrels of oil spilled over areas of the sea in the west. A large number of people volunteered to clean up the spill and Christians actively participated in this effort. At this time, progressive and conservatives churches together announced a statement on environmental preservation.

Churches began paying attention to food. Churches considered the pollution of food to be the pollution of human conscience and at the same time, the pollution of modern civilization. Food became a means of making profit and food safety was not guaranteed. The cooperative movement emerged in this context. The Christian Association of the Environmental Movement began the Life Table Campaign with churches. This campaign included producing and buying healthy and safe food, making simple meals and generating no food waste. It challenged Christians and at the same time touched their hearts. Many Christians seriously considered daily meals as their participation in Holy Communion and changed their ideas about consuming and eating food. They agreed to the idea that buying healthy, organic food could contribute to the life of organic farmers, the restoration of land, the life of all creatures and eventually the preservation of God's creation.

There are now many life & peace campaigns going on such as the green shop campaign based on the idea of resource recycling, the green church campaign based on God's creation and human duties, and the public transportation use campaign to slow down global warming. A campaign to reduce energy consumption and increase alternative energy development, a tree planting campaign to prevent desertification in Mongolia and a seminar on ecological pastoral care are also being carried out by different groups of Christians.

Churches have articulated their positions based on deep insights and considerations in difficult times. In 1973, churches protested against the military dictatorship and urged the country's democratization. Churches confronted Park Chunghee's long-term plan for dictatorship through the Yushin Constitution. Churches' protests and clear position statements encouraged civil organizations' resistance. In 1988, churches announced the Korean Churches' Statement on Peace and Reunification of the Korean Peninsula. This statement provided the government with a foundation for reunification policies. In 2010, churches announced a statement on life and peace. Churches involved in social missions now regard life and peace as their central values, and they work to encourage churches to embrace the values of life and peace. Life and peace are two of the most important Christian values in this era. Churches have a duty to bring together all the entities and organizations that share the value of life and peace, and to make efforts to overcome the market economy based on neo-liberalism and build a community of humans and other creatures based on mutual respect and peaceful co-existence.